KW-222-399

A Mirror for Simple Souls

GILL'S SPIRITUAL CLASSICS

Series Editor: JOHN GRIFFITHS

WITHDRAWN FROM STOCK

This series introduces the general reader to works from the various Christian traditions of spirituality which are of enduring value and interest but not generally accessible. It will include some well-known works which will gain a new lease of life from a fresh translation or adaptation, but the emphasis will be on texts not available in any modern English version.

All the works chosen have more than historical interest. They can speak to men and women of today in ways that will often be unexpected, often challenging, never dull. The introduction to each text helps bring the past to life by setting the author (where known) and the work in their cultural, social and historical context, and relating them to streams of thought and belief that, often unconsciously, still influence our beliefs and behaviour today.

The translations and adaptations are responsibly made from the best manuscripts and existing editions, with the prime concern being to present spiritual treasures from past ages in good, direct modern English. Period charm may on occasions be a consideration, but is never allowed to override contemporary effectiveness. The author's message is given precedence without destroying the meaning of the text.

Stripped of difficult and alienating linguistic quirks – of their own time and of other versions, most of them made in the eighteenth or nineteenth centuries – these works show a continuity of vision that makes them contemporary. In this form, they are not of yesterday, but of their time and ours.

Cartlann Leabharlann Luimneach

Uniform with this volume
A Letter of Private Direction
  A 14th-century English mystic
The Cell of Self-knowledge
  Early English mystical treatises
A Letter from Jesus Christ
  John of Landsberg

A MIRROR FOR SIMPLE SOULS

by
a French mystic of the
thirteenth century

GILL AND MACMILLAN

Coláiste
Mhuire Gan Smal
Luimneach
Class No. 2 × 2   MIR
Acc. No. 100417

12238

First published 1981
in Ireland, the UK and associated territories by
GILL AND MACMILLAN LTD
Goldenbridge, Inchicore, Dublin
with associated companies in
London, New York, Delhi, Hong Kong, Johannesburg,
Lagos, Singapore, Melbourne, Tokyo

Edited, translated and adapted by Charles Crawford
Translation and Introduction Copyright © 1981 by Charles
Crawford

All rights reserved. No part of this publication
may be reproduced in any form, quoted or used in any way
for any purpose without the previous written permission of
Process Workshop Ltd, 28–32 Shelton St, London WC2H 9HP

ISBN: 7171 1158 X

Designed and produced by Process Workshop Ltd, London
Photoset by Keyspools Ltd, Golborne, Lancs.
Reproduced from copy supplied
and printed in Great Britain by
Billing & Sons Ltd,
Guildford, London, Oxford, Worcester

Contents

A Note on the Illustrations

The Frontispiece, here representing the simple soul passing unscathed through temptations, is from a woodcut in Felix Hemmerlin, *Opuscula et Tractatus* (Strasbourg, after 1497).

The 'dialoguing figures' on the versos of the openings of Parts One and Two, are from a woodcut by Michael Wolgemut showing angels praising God on the first day of creation, from the *Nuremberg Chronicles* (Latin edition, 1493). The church towers, here symbolizing the aspirations of the soul, are from the same source.

The 'Author' on the verso of the opening of Part Three is from a woodcut in *Augustinus, De civitate Dei*, printed by Johannes Amerbach (Basle, 1489).

The tailpiece is a printer's device from Book V of the *Revelationum Caelestium Sanctae Brigittae de Suetia* (1680).

The editor would like to express his thanks to the Librarian of Heythrop College, London, for supplying sources for the Frontispiece, 'Author' and tailpiece.

Introduction

The unknown author of this remarkable work – here published for only the second time in any version – is reaching out beyond the spirituality of medieval monasticism, in which the routine of the cloister, the deliberate effort to perform mundane tasks for the greater glory of God, was of paramount importance. His book, which the censors to whom he submitted it (see pp. 23–4) counselled him to keep 'for a few readers', takes such a spirituality as a lowly rung on the ladder of the ascent to perfection: all 'outward works' are something to be sloughed off at an early stage. He is writing for those who seek to pass beyond the service of God into the very existence of God. In this he is adding his – significant – contribution to a tradition of mystical writing stretching back to early Christian times, whose concern is to discover and describe the means by which God makes himself known to his creatures.

This is done through a twin movement of understanding and love: sometimes one is dominant, sometimes the other, but they are basically inseparable in the classical mystic tradition. The impulse for this twin movement comes from 'the soul' and from God himself, but there comes a point at which the soul must recognize its inability to progress further through any act of will and has to cast its aspirations wholly on God. This occurs between the third and fourth stages of the seven stages of ascent summarized by 'the Soul' in the penultimate chapter.

The stress is all on the *personal* quest of the soul for a deep *personal* relationship direct with God (service to fellow-Christians has a very low priority in this soul's view – though one must bear in mind the original translator's reminders that the soul is speaking only of her moments of rapture and has all the 'ordinary' virtues under her control all the time). The development of this quest follows a strict method which by the thirteenth century had developed a long literary tradition; this was to go on developing till it reached its maximum degree of exposition and commentary in St John of the Cross three centuries later.

With minor variations, this codification of the mystical experience derives from a small body of writings known as the *Corpus Areopagiticum*, which until the sixteenth century were almost universally believed to be the 'secret writings' of St Paul's Athenian convert, Dionysius, or Denis, the Areopagite. Though these writings were later assigned to the fifth or sixth centuries (and their author consequently demoted as the 'Pseudo-Dionysius'), their supposed near-apostolic authorship gave them an extraordinary degree of authority throughout the Middle Ages. It would be possible to argue that this single body of writings did more than any other to turn the attention of some of the most brilliant and devout minds of Christendom away from the central message of the New Testament for centuries, and to domesticate the perennial gnostic temptation just enough to keep it (though not always) within the accepted bounds of Christian orthodoxy. Had those later writers most influenced by the Pseudo-Dionysius been more aware of his true provenance, they might well have been more wary of making such extended use of his main themes.

The *Corpus* deals with the question of how God can be linked with his creation, how he can be known in it and how he shares his life with it. The way in which the divine relationship with creation is expressed is also highly relevant in terms of later developments in thinking about the nature of the Church and society, since the form in which God participates in his creation is through a series of hierarchies, the *Celestial Hierarchies* and the *Ecclesiastical Hierarchies* (the titles of two treatises in the *Corpus*). In true neo-Platonic manner, the celestial ones above are the 'intelligible realities' which are reflected in the terrestial ones below.

Pseudo-Dionysian responsibility for the perpetuation of the notion of the Church as a hierarchically ordained society would be another endless avenue of exploration, but, more relevantly, not only the basic doctrine, but also the structure and language of the *Mirror*, derive from the *Corpus* and its medieval progeny. Numerically-influenced concepts such as the soul's six wings in imitation of the seraphim, and later the 'three hard answers', have their ultimate origin in it, as would the theology underlying the strange illustration of a host being pounded in a mortar (p. 52). But this is the negative side of Dionysius' influence, and there is a positive side, of deeper importance. This derives from the most genuinely Christian emphasis in the *Corpus*, found in the treatise on the Divine Names (*de divinis nominibus*) and the short treatise on *Mystical Theology*[1] which follows it. Here Dionysius develops the notion of the voluntary goodness of God as the only means of access to him, which is the basic theme of the *Mirror*. This underlying 'goodness' ('bounty' in the first translation) shows itself in God's yearning to give himself to his creatures, and to be loved by them in return. This divine 'esctasy' (*ekstasis* – standing outside) is reciprocated in the ecstasy felt by the soul, and the basic endeavour of the author of the *Mirror* is to describe this reciprocal process of the soul moving outside ('without') itself and into God, and God moving into the soul.

The process to union beyond this mutual ecstasy, involving first the abandonment of all sense experience, then of all 'spiritual experience' ('It is far harder to master the will of the spirit than it is to master the will of the body in order to do the will of the spirit'), and then the willingness to abandon even the love that follows from this, if such be the will of God, is described in *Mystical Theology* and taken up and developed in particular in the Victorine school of spiritual writing, whose works are the immediate predecessors of the *Mirror*. Founded by William of Champeaux, the school of the Chapter of St Victor, at the gates of Paris, produced a series of treatises that were to influence all later spiritual writers. Hugh of St

Victor, who succeeded William of Champeaux as Master of the school in 1133, fused, in his life and in his writings, the functions of learning and contemplation. Theology for him was no abstract science, but the 'art of reforming the soul and leading her to salvation'. He wrote a commentary on the *Celestial Hierarchies*, in which he stresses the primacy of love, and the treatise *De Contemplatione et eius speciebus* (which stands as a summary of his thought even it is not certainly by his hand) takes up the passion for symbolic numbers characteristic of Pseudo–Dionysius and reflected in the *Mirror*: so there are 'seven sendings', 'three paradises', 'six bonds', 'four inspirations', etc. He describes the mystical state in terms that prefigure the imagery of the last chapters of the *Mirror*, with their emphasis on hatred of sin and total renunciation of all material and spiritual props: 'In that blessed sight, the few who have the happiness of enjoying it in this present life are ravished by the extreme sweetness of tasting God, and no longer look at anything but God . . . The whole soul is lit up with the splendour of eternal light; it hates sin with a constant and absolute hatred, puts the world into the background, renounces itself, and tends wholly towards God, . . . freed from matter, stripped of all form, freed from every limitation.' For him, as for the author of the *Mirror*, the goal of Christian life is union with God in love – though he likewise stresses that it is given only to very few to enjoy this in this life – and he illustrates this with the imagery of 'spiritual nuptials' derived from the *Song of Songs* that was to reappear in virtually all later mystical writing and find its most beautiful expression in the poems of St John of the Cross.

Hugh was followed by the even more famous and influential Richard of St Victor, who became Prior in 1162 and died in 1173. It is probably from his treatise *De Trinitate* that the *Mirror* takes its emphasis on the life of the Trinity as the ultimate object of contemplation, not to say participation in the life of the Trinity as the ultimate aim of life. In particular, this treatise taught that the Trinity itself derives its necessary plurality from love, so that the 'procession' of the Son from the Father is one of love, rather than one of knowledge, as in St Augustine. So the soul's journey to contemplation must equally be one of love: wounded by original sin, the will of the soul can nevertheless regain its initial purity and reach God. His *De quatuor gradibus violentae caritatis*, as well as adding more symbolic arithmetic, spells out the heights and depths of the way to perfection in terms strongly reminiscent of the *Mirror*. His *Benjamin* treatises[2] describe six degrees of contemplation (the pattern reflected in the *Mirror*, chapter 8 – the seventh being after this life), deepening according to the degree of dignity of their object, the higher stages of which can be reached by grace (God's 'goodness' or 'bounty') alone. Richard's influence on all later spiritual writers was immense, and in particular opened up the way to the 'speculative mysticism' of the fourteenth-century Rhineland mystics, which to an extent the author of the *Mirror* prefigures – to the alarm of his original translator.

The place occupied by the Pseudo–Dionysius in the

mystical theology of the Victorines is emphasized by the fact that Thomas of St Victor (also known as Thomas Gallus), devoted most of his intellectual endeavour to commentaries on the *Corpus Areopagiticum*. In this he stresses the importance of total renunciation, the absolute 'emptiness of the understanding as a condition of union with God', which leads directly to the development of the concept of the 'dark night' in the *Mirror*, and further on to the anti-intellectual tendency of the *Cloud of Unknowing*, the negative theology of the Rhineland mystics and the whole 'Quietist' tendency. So the influence of the Victorines is a major channel by which the ideas of the Pseudo-Dionysius became the staple diet of spiritual writers of the Middle Ages and after.

The *Mirror* occupies a significant place in this tradition, not least for its development of the concept of the 'dark night', which accounts for some of its most telling passages. It would be wrong to give the impression that this is academic writing simply following a precedent. It is obviously based on personal experience and written from an overwhelming urge to try to communicate the essentially incommunicable. The passages describing the successive 'dark nights' (of the senses and then of the soul: 'far night' in the original, which is perhaps an even more compelling image, though the more familiar term has been preferred here) are central to the book and contain some of its most obviously heartfelt writing and – more importantly – its densest reasoning. A glimpse of the agonizing struggle out of which this reasoning evolved can be found in the most dramatic part of the book, the autobiographical final chapter, in which the author, still in the person of 'the free Soul', describes his own progress to the point of absolute surrender to the heart and will of God, reached through acceptance of three final terrible suppositions about God's will:

—Suppose you wanted me to love someone else more than you . . .

—Suppose you wanted to love someone else more than you love me . . .

—Suppose you wanted someone else to love me more than you . . .

Faced with these, any lover's heart might well quail in purely human terms, let alone in divine ones. But here, surely, is the point at which all the somewhat élitist theology which forms one of the main literary strands of the *Mirror* falls away, and we can see that under the playful form and the scholastic debate, the author is tackling central facets of human existence with real passion and sincerity. Whatever terms the Beloved who can put such a challenge is seen in, it is a challenge of love and to love, and love is God and God is love, and the only answer must be: 'I still love you for yourself and in yourself'.

* * *

There is no known copy of the French original of the *Mirror*, and any new version has to rely on the three known copies of the English translation,[3] all of which belong to the latter part of the fifteenth century, and one of which shows some variants from the other two and appears to have been based on an older version of the French original. There is also a translation into

Latin, made by Richard Methley in the late fifteenth
century from one of the English versions, and there
are four other known Latin translations, apparently
made from the lost French original, and one Italian
MS. Methley's Latin version attributes the original to
Ruysbroeck, but internal evidence (the dates of the
censors to whom it was sent) makes this impossible.

The manuscripts of the translation seem to have
lain virtually unnoticed in various libraries from the
end of the fifteenth century till the beginning of the
twentieth, when the then keeper of MSS at the British
Museum brought it to the attention of Evelyn
Underhill in 1911. She published an account of it in
the *Fortnightly Review* and some extracts in *The Porch*
in the same year. It was published in its entirety for
the first and, till now, only time in an edition made by
Clare Kirchenberger for the 'Orchard Books' series of
spiritual classics, in 1927.[4] The concern of this edition
was evidently, and quite correctly, mainly to establish
the most authentic reading of the text, taking account
of the variant readings in the different MSS. Though
the editor translated old terms considered inaccessible
to a twentieth-century readership, she kept as closely
to the original as was consistent with intelligibility,
and her version does not make for easy reading today.
The aim of the present version, in keeping with that of
this series, is somewhat different: simply to bring out
the essence of the original in simple modern English.

The dialogue form in which the book is couched,
which owes something to the 'disputation' of
thirteenth-century scholasticism, but more to the
poetic tournaments or *Jeu-partis* popular at the time,

has been retained and, it is hoped, enhanced by the direct speech form adopted here.

The MSS are divided into 'Divisions' and these are further sub-divided in the Bodley MS into short chapters, with summaries at the head of each. Here the Divisions have, in the main, been kept as Chapters, with the Bodley chapter summaries, much simplified, used as sub-headings within the chapters. The division into three Parts follows Clare Kirchenberger's analysis of the structure of the book. Part Two, which in the original gives the impression of being a collection of short pieces not too rigorously pruned to fit into the main argument of the book, and tends to recapitulate to the point of tedium, has been considerably shortened so as to bring out its main thrust.

One of the most delightful features of the *Mirror* as it has been preserved is the way the original English translator interpolates his own comments where he feels the need to do so, generally because a doctrinal point seems so close to the heterodox as expressed that he feels an explanation is needed in order to protect the faith of his readers. His humble but sensible interjections provide an additional voice of reason and relate what is essentially an account of the life of prayer to the realities of everyday life. In the MSS, his comments are opened and closed by his initials M and N (which have not proved enough of a clue to establish his identity). Here, as *Translator*, he has been promoted to the rank of another participant in the dialogue, since his voice, despite his own protestations of inadequacy, is worthy of at least as much attention as the others. His own spirituality, as it appears from his comments, suggests that he may have been a disciple of Walter Hilton, and his language suggests that he came from the North Midlands of England. Whoever he was, he shows a fine understanding of his trade, and his Prologue contains a statement of the principles he followed which can well stand to excuse the liberties taken in the present version: 'Translation . . . is a matter of conveying the sense of the original, not of finding an exact equivalent for each word.'

Charles Crawford

Notes

1. Trans. by the author of *The Cloud of Unknowing*, in *A Letter of Private Direction and other treatises*, ed. J. Griffiths, in this series (Dublin & New York, 1981), pp. 77–91.

2. Trans. in *A Letter . . .*, *op. cit.*, pp. 93–122.

3. British Museum, MS Adds. 37790; Bodleian Library, Oxford, 505; St John's College Library, Cambridge, 71.

4. *The Mirror of Simple Souls*, by an unknown French mystic of the thirteenth century, Translated into English by M.N., now first edited from the MSS by Clare Kirchenberger (Orchard Books XV, London, 1927).

Translator's prologue

I first undertook to translate *A Mirror for Simple Souls* – despite my limited talents and lack of learning – from the French a good many years ago, believing it would prove spiritually beneficial to all who might read it. I have now been told that some of its statements are ambiguous, so I have reworked it to make them clearer. They are made in the book by *Love*, but briefly, and in terms open to misunderstanding. I have therefore – in some trepidation, since the book speaks of the highest matters concerning the soul in the subtlest of language – provided a gloss on some of these statements, thinking that if they are spelt out twice in slightly different words they will be easier to understand. I do not claim to be the equal of the author in this respect, and believe I know my own failings, but trust in the goodness of Jesus to enlighten my mind and keep me on the right track.

To the readers of the book, I would echo David's 'Taste and see'. Why taste first? The soul needs to taste before her understanding is opened to sight of the workings of the love of God. Without this taste, writings that try to speak of it will be arid and bitter to the soul. But once the soul has learnt through grace to then she will appreciate the fare being set before her here, and long to have more and more of it.

At this point the soul is beginning on the illuminative way, starting to see how the mind of God works. This is a necessary preparation for the unitive way, in which the soul drowns in the flood of divine love, a bride united to her bridegroom. This book is a work of Love designed to help the soul on this path. But such matters cannot always be laid open at first glance; they are a precious kernel hidden under an outer shell. So the depths of this book are hidden under clouds, as it were; readers must uncover them as best they may to reach the kernel of love. *Love* also in these pages sometimes addresses her remarks to three different audiences: actives, contemplatives and ordinary people. Even so, her meaning has been misunderstood, as I said, so I have added a gloss where this seemed necessary, as best I could, taking care to show clearly in the text where my own words begin and end.

The French manuscript I have translated is difficult to read and has words missing in places. Translation, furthermore, is a matter of conveying the sense of the original, not of finding an exact equivalent for each word. This, God willing, I have tried to do to the best of my ability. In all things I submit myself to the judgment of Holy Church, and ask those more wise and learned than myself to correct any faults they may find.

May Christ Our Lord help me now to bring this translation to a worthy conclusion.

Author's prologue

As I am a creature of God's, so I humbly offer this book as a creature of mine. So I submit it, in the hope that it conveys something of the wisdom and love of God, who is Three in One, to the judgment of those who will give approval to it. It has already been read and approved by three men of learning and holiness.

The first of these was a Franciscan friar known for the goodness of his life, Bro. John of Querayn, who wrote: 'I write in *Love*, trusting in the *Courtesy* of your reading of my letter: it is Love's prayer that all may come to worship God and find freedom in him; that he may enable those who have not yet reached this point to do so.' He went on – and I believe he spoke truly – that the book is really the work of the Holy Spirit, and that if it is understood this will be due to the working of that Spirit, not to the learning of the readers. This means, he said, that its inspiration is not for all; those incapable of understanding it should have it kept from them. He added that he was not sure that he himself understood it all.

The second was a Cistercian monk, Dom Frank, Cantor of the Abbey of Villiers. He found it to be in full accord with the Scriptures, and true in all things it said.

The third was a theologian, Godfrey of Fountains. He found no fault in it, but also advised that it should be kept to a few readers, so as not to disturb those who had found their own spiritual path and encourage them to forsake ways that suited them better than the way put forward in these pages, which might not be apt for them. Its words cut deep, and can only be appreciated by the few who have advanced beyond the early stages of the way of perfection. They can only come there through God's action, not their own: this is the way God works.

I obtained these approbations, readers, for your peace of mind. May it add to your peace of mind if I say finally that if you are capable of reading these words, then they will bear good fruit in your soul.

PART ONE

A *dialogue*
between *Love* and *Reason*
(with other characters)
concerning the ascent of the ladder
of perfection

Coláiste Oideachais Mhuire Gan Smál
100417
Luimneach

CHAPTER ONE

How this book is to be understood

An initial word of encouragement

You, soul, have known the divine touch, been set apart from sin in the first stage of grace; may divine grace lead you to the seventh stage, in which the soul reaches the fulness of perfection in the peace of the love of God. You activists and contemplatives who aspire to this stage, listen now to some hint of the bright, noble and highest love that is found in the souls of those set free, and of how the Holy Spirit steers the ship of the soul into the calm waters of peace.

Love: I beg you, those who read these words, try to understand them inwardly, in the innermost depths of your understanding, with all the subtle powers at your command, or else you run the risk of failing to understand them at all.

Let me give you a little illustration: it tells of worldly love, but you should take it in terms of divine love.

Once upon a time there was a princess in a far off country, a lady of great worth and virtue. She heard tell of the chivalry and generosity of King Alexander, and fell in love with him by repute. But she lived far away from him, with no hope of ever seeing him or being with him. This was a cause of great distress to her, for no other love would she have. So to make up for the fact that her love – who seemed so close to her – was so far away, she sought to comfort herself by having an image made in the likeness of him whose image was graven on her heart. So she had a picture painted, as accurate a portrait as could be made, and by gazing on this, no doubt with many a sigh, she consoled herself for the absence of the original.

So, as writer of this book, I find myself in much the same case as this princess. The king of whom I speak is above Alexander even in chivalry and generosity. But he is so far from me and I am so far from him, that I am in distress. So he inspired me to write this book, which gives some inkling of the practice of his love. But it is only a semblance, and leaves me in a far country, far from the kingdom of his peace, in which those who love this king with pure perfection, those to whom he has given the gift of perfect freedom, dwell. If we are to reach this kingdom, it will not be through our own nobility and freedom but through his love which sets us free.

Translator: Readers, heed these words: 'not ... our own nobility and freedom'. We cannot be wholly free as long as we remain in this world, because we cannot remain free from all stain of sin. But when your soul is drawn away from all outside things, into herself, her inner being where love can work on her – which takes her away from all stain of sin for the time being and unites her in union with God – then for a time (for that time of union, however short it may be), the soul can be said to be free. Once back from that state of union, the soul is back in bondage. This will happen again and again, for as the Scriptures say: 'The virtuous man falls seven times' (Prov. 24: 26). But this is a merit, not a failing, and does not change the will to be united again to God.

So, while you may always enjoy the freedom brought by grace, you cannot expect always to be free from sin; we are all subject to fleeting urges to sensuality, at least. But the failing is in the sensuality, not in the will shown by the soul that has set its sights on God, whose love will set it free. This is what is meant by saying that it is not 'our own nobility and freedom', but his love that sets us free.

So now let me tell you something of how love can conquer all. Love will show us six ways to nobility of soul; how we must have being before we can be perfect. This will be explained in the course of this book, whose purpose is to show the ways love works.

The book is for those who seek the perfection necessary for salvation

Love: I have made this book for you children of Holy Mother Church who seek perfection and peace, which come through the exercise of perfect charity. This is God's gift, and I will explain to the questioning reason how it is to be obtained.

We can begin with the commandment to love: to love God with all our heart and all our soul and in all our deeds, to love ourselves in due measure and our fellow Christians as ourselves. To love God with all our heart means keeping our thoughts for ever fixed on him; to love him with our whole soul means with our very life, speaking always the truth about him; in all our deeds means that we should do everything for his sake. Loving ourselves in due measure means that we look for his will, not ours, to be done in us. Loving our fellows as ourselves means that we should do to them as we would have them do to us. All these aspects of the commandment are necessary for our salvation, and if we do not observe them, we will not have grace living in us.

Perfection and praise of charity

A rich young man came to Jesus and asked what he must do to inherit eternal life, saying he had kept the commandments from his earliest days. Jesus told him there was one thing he still lacked: 'Go and sell everything you own and give the money to the poor, and you will have treasure in heaven; then come, follow me' (Mk. 10: 21). This is a counsel of perfection in virtue, and those who carry it out live in charity.

Charity owns no master but love, possesses nothing and asks nothing for herself; looks after others, not herself, asking nothing in return; she knows neither shame nor fear nor unease, flinching from nothing that might befall her.

Charity takes no heed of anything under the sun; the whole world is her domain. She gives freely to all anything she may possess of value, her own self included. Her generosity can lead her to promise things she does not possess, yet she is shrewd enough to win where others lose out. Her works lead to the highest degrees of the spiritual life, and to perfection in charity.

CHAPTER TWO

Nine features of the soul

There is also another mode of being which we can call the peace of love in a life brought to nothingness.

Love: These are its features, and we will then ask a soul to describe them for us:
- No one can find her;
- She is saved by faith alone;
- She is alone in love;
- She does nothing for God;
- She leaves nothing to God;
- She cannot be taught;
- She cannot be robbed;
- She cannot be given anything;
- She has no will.

This soul, like the seraphim, has six wings, and, also like them, wants nothing that comes through a go-between. It is the nature of the seraphim to have no intermediary between their love and God's love, and to know everything directly. The same is true of the soul that does not look to the world for understanding of God, but despises the world and herself. You, Lord, know how great a difference there is between the love that comes through a go-between and the love that comes direct from the beloved.

The soul's six wings and what they do

I meant it when I said the soul had six wings, and this is what they do: Two cover the face of Our Lord, which means that the more the soul knows of divine goodness, the more it knows that it knows nothing of it, which only God himself can understand. Two cover his feet, which means that the more the soul knows of Jesus' sufferings, the more it knows that it knows nothing of them, which only he can know. Two enable it to fly into the company of God, there to dwell in the goodness of his will.

So what need the soul fear, even though she remains in this world, with the flesh and the devil to tempt her, the elements and the birds of the air and the beasts of the field to torment her, as long as God is with her? For is he not almighty, all wise, all good, our Father, our brother and best friend, without beginning and without end? None but he can encompass him, eternal three-in-one, the soul's beloved.

Beyond the virtues

Love: Once a soul has reached this state, she can say to the virtues: 'I have no further need of you, now I have served you all this time'.

The Soul: I agree, Love: I was their servant, but now you have set me free from them. Virtues, goodbye! My heart is now freer and more at peace than it has ever been. It was hard work being your servant, obeying you in everything. In fact it's a wonder I'm still alive, but I need worry no more, since I am now beyond your control and can live in peace.

Translator: Love may say simply that the soul has no further need of virtues, but I really think some explanation is called for. As I see it, it means this: When the soul is striving for perfection, she seeks constantly to obtain virtues through the use of reason, and in the same way to blot out vices. So the virtues are mistresses of the soul, and at war within her with their enemies the vices. This war is painful and distressing to the soul, not only in the realm of conscience, but also in that of bodily constraints – fasts, abstinence from pleasures and so on – which can be just as painful. These constraints are put on the soul by her mistresses, the virtues, so it is natural that she should blame them for the pain. You have to bite hard into a bitter fruit to reach the sweet kernel.

When the soul says she can live in peace, she means that she has passed through this experience, has bitten through to the sweet kernel of God's love. Once this has been tasted, and God's love deeply implanted in the soul, then the memories of the struggle and bitterness that went before are quite blotted out. Then the soul is no longer servant of the virtues, but is in charge of them, and can command them without feeling any pain. So she can claim properly to be beyond their control, for now it is the soul that is in control of them, and in this sense 'has no further need' of them. I hope this is now clearer.

Things the soul does not know

Love: This soul knows neither shame nor honour, neither poverty nor riches, neither leisure nor cares, neither love nor hate, neither heaven nor hell.

35

Reason: For God's sake, Love, what can you mean?

Love: What I mean can only be understood by those God has given understanding; you will not find it in the textbooks, nor can human reason work it out. It is a gift from the Almighty, in whom all knowing leads to loss of understanding.

Translator: To say that all knowing leads to a loss of understanding in the Almighty must surely strike the reader as strange – and it's not the first thing in this book that sounds a bit far-fetched, and I fear it won't be the last! But please, gentle reader, be patient; I am sure that when you have read this book carefully two or three times in sympathy with its aims, you will understand it well enough. Even if you don't find yourself in sympathy with them, you will have to admit they have been well put. And you know how easy it is to fall into error by taking the words of Scripture at their face value and failing to see the deeper meaning behind them.

Love: So this soul that has become nothing knows all and knows nothing, wills everything and wills nothing.

Reason: My dear Lady, you said before that this soul has no will. How then can she will everything and nothing?

Love: Because, dear Reason, it not the soul's will that wills, but God's will willing in her; the soul does not take the lead in loving, but lets Love lead and take over her will, and have his will of her.

So now love can work in the soul without the soul's will, and the soul will be free from all cares.

Freed from all desires, the soul cannot even speak of God. An explanation of 'beyond the virtues'

Love: Once the soul is stripped of all desires, physical or spiritual, she can no longer even speak of God. Her actions are now guided by her good habits – or by the teaching of the Church – since she has no more will, and therefore no desires.

Reason (eager to understand, but not seeing the point): Surely this is not so strange? If this soul has been deprived of a feeling of grace, of all desires, physical and spiritual, isn't this because she has decided to take leave of the virtues? Surely without them no one can be saved, or reach perfection, or be safe from deception? Yet this soul has taken leave of them: is she out of her mind?

Love: No, absolutely not. She has more virtues than anyone else, but she has lost the practice of them, because she does not *pursue* them like she used to. She was their servant for a long time, and now, God willing, is free of them.

Reason: When was she their servant?

Love: When she took the initiative in love, and in obeying you and the other virtues. After taking the initiative for so long, such souls are set free.

Reason: When are they set free?

Love: When love takes the lead with them, and takes them over, the virtues serve them; though they cannot know this is happening nor does it cause them any distress.

Reason: So these souls that are set free have long known what it is to be under outside control, and if anyone were to ask them what the greatest torment a creature can suffer is, they would answer: 'To take the initiative in love and in obeying the virtues', because then you have to give the virtues everything they ask for, whatever the cost in denying your nature, and they ask for everything: your fame, your honour, your heart, your body, your life. So once a soul has given them all this, she has precious little left to comfort herself with this side of judgment day, and will suffer the torments of hell till then. But once there, she knows she's saved.

Love: That's true. Those the virtues have such power over live under outside control. But the souls I am talking about have made their virtues perfect; they no longer serve the virtues but make them do what they want, since they have become their mistresses.

What free souls do without will

If anyone were to ask such souls whether they would like to be in Purgatory, they would answer 'No'; if they would like to be certain of salvation while still in this world, again 'No'; if they would rather be in Paradise, 'No! What can you mean?' They have no will to want such things, and if they had, they would be falling short of love. Their will is possessed by Him who is; he knows what is good for them, and they are content with this, without any further knowledge, let alone certainty. Knowledge of love is sufficient for them, and this is how they exist. With this knowledge and love dwelling in them, they cannot tell good from evil, nor know by themselves whether they will be saved or lost.

One soul as an example, and God's greatest gift to his creatures

Love: Let's take one soul as an example: she seeks neither disgrace nor poverty, worries nor cares; she needs no masses or sermons, or fasting or prayers; she gives nature all she asks willingly and ungrudgingly.

Translator: I take this to mean that this soul is in union with God, and while in that state of union, wants nothing, does nothing and thinks of nothing except that union. But it can also mean this: that when people set their hearts on becoming perfect, their whole attention is concentrated on the things Love lists. So for God's sake they seek trials and poverty; they seek out masses and sermons; they fast and they pray; they deprive nature of her wants – i.e., the desires of the flesh. This is the way of mortification through which the soul must pass before she knows God's way. But once the heady wine of God's love has been tasted, everything else loses its savour. His love makes the soul stop having to try, but this does not mean that she gives up good practices. God's light and love show her that they are worth more to her than the labours on which she set her heart before, so that all

39

her attention is concentrated away from outward works and on following the dictates of love. But this does not mean abandoning the outward works: as Love has said earlier: 'Her actions are now guided by her good habits'. But she no longer has to strive to do them, and can put her whole being in the hands of love, which will bear her up to God. Whatever she does, is love's doing. So when Love says that this soul 'needs no masses or sermons, or fasting or prayer', this does not mean that the person never goes to mass, listens to a sermon, fasts or prays! You would have to be blind to take it like this: everything in this book must be seen as having a spiritual meaning. Such a soul humbles herself to the point of seeing herself as a non-person, because sin is a non-thing, and she sees herself as sin, so sees herself as doing no-thing, but God doing everything in her. Such souls also have no will or desires, as these are wholly set on God, so that nothing of them is left but what God wills and desires in them.

When Love says that this soul gives nature 'all she asks willingly and ungrudgingly', you must not think that this means giving in to the lusts of the flesh: God knows, it can't mean that! Sin requires the assent of conscience, whether you know it or not at the time. Anyone of good sense realizes this, and the souls described in this book have been through such mortification and been so enlightened by grace, and dwell so perfectly in the love of God, that all bodily lusts have been extinguished in them, as have all spiritual temptations. So Love, which means the Holy Spirit, works in such people, makes her dwelling in them, adorns them with the garlands of her generosity, so that no spot nor blemish can any longer be found in them.

(*Love continues:*) She is not worried about anything she lacks, except in her time of need. Only the innocent can escape the weight of this burden.

Reason: In God's name, what do you mean?

Love: I have already told you, but I'll tell you again, that neither your greatest philosophers, nor biblical scholars, nor those who pursue love and the virtues, can understand this, but only those who are guided by true love. If you could find any of these, they could tell you, if they would, but it's not my job to make everyone understand – only those who are guided by true love. To be so guided is a gift that can come in an instant, and anyone who receives it had better hold on to it, for it is God's greatest gift to his creatures. Such a soul is like a divinity scholar who must cross the valley of humility and the plain of truth before climbing the mountain of love and there finding rest.

Reason: That's all very well for scholars, Love, but tell us 'activists' what this soul is in terms we can understand.

So Love does. She calls it: truly marvellous; unknown; the most innocent of the daughters of Jerusalem; the Church's foundation; enlightened by knowledge; honoured by love; united in hearing; denied through humility; at peace in divine being, through divine will, willing nothing of herself; fulfilled; unfailingly called by divine goodness, through the Trinity; forgetful.

41

Translator: 'Forgetful', since she understands a lot and forgets it; understanding when she sees the goodness and glory of God, his power and might in his works, how he is all in all, good and merciful, forgiving and gentle in all his doings. In understanding this, she is often wounded so sweetly by the darts of divine love that all understanding is swept away from her. She also understands in the moment of being united to God, then instantly forgets herself and all she knew before. So she understands a lot and soon forgets it.

These are the names Love gives her, and surely they are right.

Reason: Yes, Love, those are many names by which activists might at least come to have some idea of her. Now give us something for the contemplatives, who always seek to increase their knowledge of God's goodness.

Love: I doubt if you will get them to listen to you, Reason.

Translator: This means that the contemplatives should not always be 'seeking', but should have no other desires other than the will of God. They should have gone beyond the stage of scholarly enquiry, just as professors should have advanced beyond college.

Nine features of the soul mentioned before: the first feature

Reason: Now, Love, be so good as to explain – for those contemplatives whose desire is fixed on the love of God – the nine features of the soul you mentioned before, the one that is sought out by love, in whom love dwells, who lives humbled in this life so as to be melted into pure love. The first of these features was that no one can find her.

Love: Yes, this means that all the soul knows of herself is that she is the root of all evil, sin without number; as sin has no weight nor measure, it is nothing and less than nothing. So this soul feels herself to be less than nothing, and there is nothing of her to be found, as she is so humbled by her meekness that she sees herself as worthy of God's punishment for but a thousandth part of her sins. Such humility is true and profitable in a soul humbled to this degree, but not in others.

The second feature: the soul saved by faith alone

Reason: Now, Love, tell us what this might mean.

Love: This means that a soul so humbled knows herself so well through faith that she must bear in herself all the knowledge acquired through faith of the power of the Father, the wisdom of the Son and the goodness of the Spirit. No intellectual concepts can remain long in her, but pass fleetingly through, since this humbled soul lives in another mansion. She cannot work any more, since faith without works shows her that God is good, without her needing to put her understanding to work. So she is saved by faith alone, without works, since faith surpasses all works through the witness of the Spirit.

Translator: The Scriptures indeed tell us that 'the upright man will live by his faithfulness' (Hab. 2:4), and Love tells us these souls do the same. But her 'saved by faith alone', and 'cannot work any more', should not be taken as meaning that such people can just sit in idleness of body and mind for the rest of their lives. What the words mean is that God lives in them and works in them and such souls allow him to work his divine acts in them. Love in this book is concerned to show how God works in them, and what he does. Such souls see their bodily works, however good, as not being important enough to save them; that is, they put their trust first and foremost in the goodness of God, not in their own actions.

The third, fourth and fifth features: alone in love, doing nothing for God and leaving nothing to God

Love: The third feature is being alone in love. This means that she can take no pleasure in anything created in heaven or on earth, but only in God's goodness. She asks nothing of other creatures, but, alone like the phoenix, she remembers only God.

The fourth is doing nothing for God.

Reason: So help me God, what can this mean?

Love: That God does not 'make a to-do' about his work, so the soul need not either. Nor can she take heed for herself, knowing that God takes care of her, and loving God so much that there is no room in her for self-love. Her faith in God is such that she need not fear being poor while she is so rich in love. Faith teaches her that as much as she hopes for from God, so much will he give her, and so she hopes to find him.

The fifth feature is leaving nothing to God that she wishes to do herself. This means that all the soul wants is God's will, so there is nothing left to God, since there is nothing in her innermost thoughts that is contrary to God and so would give God something to overcome.

The sixth and seventh features: she cannot be taught or robbed

Love: The sixth feature is that her knowledge is such that, even if she had all the learning in the world, she would esteem it as nothing compared to what she loves, which can never be known. She loves the qualities of God, ungiven and impossible to give, more than all that has been and will be given to her. All the knowledge in the world, past, present and to come, she holds as nothing compared to what is and may not be spoken.

The seventh is that she cannot be robbed. For what could men steal from her? They could take her honour, friends, life itself and yet deprive her of nothing as long as she has God in her. So all creatures are powerless against her.

The eighth feature: she cannot be given anything

In the same way, what can men give her that adds anything to what she already has in her love?

The Soul: Say rather, Love, that God loves and will love in me.

Love: That's for you to say. What I can tell the readers of this book is that God loves more where he finds more of himself in a soul than where he finds less.

The Soul: But you can't talk about there being less of God. He is himself and can't be diminished, believe me.

Love: What I am trying to say is that even if this soul had all the knowledge, all the love and all the understanding that has ever existed or will exist, this is as nothing compared to what she loves and will love, though her loved one remain forever out of reach.

The Soul: No, there is no reaching him, dear Love. The only God there is is the unknowable. Indeed, my God is the one of whom not one word can be said, whom the angels in heaven cannot begin to understand, for all their knowledge of him. All the immortal longing of my soul is taken up in contemplating him; that is what I glory in, and always shall do. I don't quite know how to say this, Love, but such is my love that I would rather hear people boast about you than hear nothing about you.

All that I say about you is really boasting, but when it's about you, it can be forgiven, because anyone who talks about you without stressing your goodness is not really talking about you properly. Not that anyone can truly grasp your goodness, but the more I hear about you, the more ashamed I am; it really hurts me when I hear people talking about your goodness: they can't know the truth of it, and so their words deceive. God willing, I shan't hear any more boasting about your divine goodness: I want no more empty talk.

Translator: Love is trying to explain – through the soul – that once the soul has attained to love of God, then all 'spiritual talk' about God seems so much empty boasting, since God's goodness can never be known or expressed; God alone can know himself. So, since there is no way these souls or others can express the fulness of the truth of God, everthing they say is empty.

The Soul (continues, addressing God): I will listen to no more boasting about your divine goodness, if I am granted life to carry out the precepts of this book, which is Love's book, and tells me to limit what I ask for, since anything asked of Love for oneself can only apply in the shadows here below, where the mystery of love in the blessed Trinity cannot be grasped.

What am I saying? Even if I possessed everything, it would be nothing compared to what I love in God, which he can give to no one but has to keep to himself. So anything creatures can give me is as nothing.

And you, Reason, try to understand what I am saying, because it comes from my heart, and once we can understand this sweet mystery, then that is Paradise.

The ninth feature: having no will

Love: This soul has no will of her own, for all that she wills is God's will for her, and she wills this in order to carry out God's will and not her own. Even this she wills not of herself but through God's will working in her, so that she has no will except the will of God which makes her will everything she ought to will.

47

Translator: Love is here saying again what she says in many places in this book, that the humbled soul has no will of her own, cannot have any, and cannot wish to have any. This is fully in accordance with the divine will. In the same way, the soul cannot have the fulness of divine love, nor can divine love fully possess the soul, until the soul is in God and God in her, when all things will be given to her.

Reason: This is fine, but it seems to contradict the ninth feature, which says that the humbled soul can will nothing about what she would like to will, and can possess nothing of what God wants her to will. And that she is indifferent to things being given to her, and that they can't be given to her and never will be.

So it seems to me that the soul wants to have a will, and God wants her to have one, but she cannot have one, and so feels deprived. So what this ninth feature seems to imply is that while the free soul has no will and cannot have one, yet all things have been given to her through the love of God.

The Soul: No, Reason, your understanding is very superficial. You just take the chaff, and leave the kernel of truth. Your understanding will never reach the heights necessary to grasp the nature of the Being we speak of. Only divine love, which guides the humbled soul set free, can truly understand it, since it is part of the divine nature.

Love: Try to see how crude your reasoning is, Reason. If this humbled soul willed the will of God, the more she did so, the more she would want to do so. But this is impossible, because the creature is of so little

48

account in relation to God, who holds back the full greatness of his goodness. But God wants her to will this, because this is the divine will, which gives life to those who are free. The divine will God puts in them draws out glimmers of divine knowledge and feelings of divine love and makes them praise the divine splendour. So how can the soul will, when the clarity of vision she is given shows her that there is a Being above all beings whom creatures cannot possess except through 'not-willing'?

So now all Reason's questions have been answered, except the point about what this soul lacks. But remember this: that if she is to will what God wills, the more she wills this, the less she takes account of her own needs, so that her will becomes wholly God's, to the glory of the soul.

Perfection according to reason, and according to true love

Reason: Now, Love, you've answered my questions for activists and contemplatives. How about explaining some of your more ambiguous terms for the ordinary people, so that they can understand something of the nature of that Being this book speaks of?

Love: I will try to do what you ask, for the sake of these 'ordinary people' you are so concerned about. But what are these ambiguous words you want me to explain for them?

Reason: You spoke earlier of the things the soul does not know: 'neither shame nor honour, neither poverty

49

nor riches, neither leisure nor cares, neither love nor hate, neither heaven nor hell'. Then, that the soul who has become nothing, 'knows all and knows nothing, wills everything and nothing'. And later, when you took one soul as an example, you said that she seeks, 'neither disgrace nor poverty, worries nor cares; she needs no masses or sermons or fasting or prayers; she gives nature all she asks willingly and ungrudgingly.' Now, surely you see that no one can understand any of this through *my* understanding. I teach people to seek disgrace and poverty and other mortifications, to go to mass, listen to sermons, fast and say their prayers, to be on their guard against nature, particularly when it tempts them to love, because you never know where that will lead. I tell them to long above all things for heaven, and to be afraid of going to hell, to refuse worldly honours and all the good things of life except what they absolutely need to survive, following the example of our Lord Jesus Christ and his sufferings.

This is the best advice I can give those who try to live by my precepts, so how can they understand this book if they follow those? Only Faith and Love, whom I have to give to way to, can help them to understand. Of course, once people have these two supports of Faith and Love, they can do what they like, as the Scriptures say: 'Love, and do what you will'.

Love: You speak well of the things that belong to you, Reason. You are quite right, and I shall try to give you a clear answer.

Once a soul is guided by true love, disgrace means

as much to her as honour, and honour as disgrace; poverty the same as riches, and riches as poverty; to be tormented by God and his creatures as to be comforted by them. It is the same to be loved as to be hated, heaven is the same as hell, and hell as heaven; wordly goods are the same as none. This means that such a soul neither desires any of these nor 'non-desires' them; her only will is God's will for her. All these things are a hindrance on the spiritual way, and once the soul is free, God removes them from her path. So, as I have said before, all manner of prosperity means as much or as little as all manner of adversity, whether of mind or body. Since she cannot pretend to understand the mind of God, why God will save her or not, why he will save other Christians or not, why God gives her the gifts he does, she has no will except to desire God's will and endure whatever he might send her.

Everything and nothing: the Trinity and the Blessed Sacrament

Reason: Please stick to my question, Love. This book says that this soul has everything and has nothing. What do you mean by this?

Love: This soul has God in her through divine grace, and whoever has God has everything. But what she has of God in her seems to her nothing compared to what she loves of God, which is in God and remains in God – the fulness of the divine life. So by realizing this, the soul has everything and nothing, knows all and knows nothing. Through faith she knows

51

everything: God is almighty, all wise, all good; he sent his Son into the world and the Son left us the Spirit, while the Son and the Holy Spirit also did the work of the Incarnation. The Father has in this way joined and united human nature to the person of the Son; the Son has joined it to himself, and the Spirit has joined it to the Son. The Father has one nature, a divine nature, whereas the Son has two natures, human and divine, and the Spirit the same divine nature. True contemplation consists in believing, saying and thinking this. God is one might, one wisdom and one will; one God in three persons and three persons in one God. His divine nature sets him above everything, but he has glorified our humanity by uniting it to the person of the Son, who is in heaven glorified and, apart from there, only in the Blessed Sacrament. So when Christians receive the sacrament, they receive the divinity and the humanity of Christ. We know through Faith how truly we receive the humanity.

Faith: But let me give you a simile to show you how to understand the humanity of Christ in the sacrament. If you take a host and pound it in a mortar with other things till no trace of it remains, it ceases to exist, since it can neither be seen nor felt. You might then ask: 'Where has it gone?'. The truth is that it was and now is not – referring to the humanity alone. So did it come as it went? The truth is that the humanity of Christ neither comes nor goes. 'How so?', doubters will ask.

Translator: This is true, that Christ's humanity neither comes nor goes. His divine power and the virtue of his word make the host become his precious body and blood. It is not that his glorious body comes down into the host, but that the host becomes him. It is thus his very body, which suffered death for our sakes – praise and thanks be his for ever. This is the way divine power ordained this sacrament.

If the saints in heaven only saw him in the host, as we do, they would see no more of him than we do. But they see through the understanding of the spirit. They see his glory through understanding; we have to rely on faith, which contradicts the evidence of our senses, which tell us that all we can see, taste or touch is bread. But faith overcomes the witness of our senses and tells us that it is not just bread, but the precious body of our Lord Jesus Christ, true God and true man. This is the light of faith, which we need, but those who are in glory do not. We, the Church on earth, are nourished by the Sacrament, so that we can know him through faith.

Although we must use our natural intelligence to try to understand this great mystery of divine love, we must not question the divine will too far. The understanding that sheds light on the soul shows her the Being she loves, enables her to draw near to and be united with him in love. She sees where she wants to make her dwelling, hears the light of knowledge telling her the glad tidings of love, and desires to become that love, so as to have only the will of him she loves.

Love: So, Reason, there is your answer. This is how the soul set free knows everything and knows nothing. Faith teaches her what she needs to know in order to be saved, but she knows nothing of what God is in himself, of himself, for himself, which is reserved to him alone. So she knows everything, and she knows nothing.

Also she wills and does not will: she wills the will of God so perfectly that she can will nothing except the will of God, imprisoned as she is by love. She wills nothing, because what she wills and what God wills in her is so little in comparison to what she would like to will, but cannot: what God ultimately wants her to will. Her will cannot be self-sufficient: this is what willing the will of God means, so that, as I said earlier, she wills everything and wills nothing.

The soul fixed on the Trinity needs nothing created

Reason: Now what about needing no masses or sermons, or fasting or prayers? Surely, Love, these are the staple diet of holy souls?

Love: That is true of those who still have spiritual cravings, but this soul is beyond these, since she has no desire for anything outside herself. God is above everything, whether one has these cravings or not. All this soul longs for is the grace of the Trinity working in her. She does not care about any sin she may have committed, nor even for Christ's sufferings for her sake, nor for the sufferings of her fellow Christians.

Reason: Now, Love, surely you're just being provocative? As you've answered my other questions, please explain this.

Love: What I mean is that these things are not her *main* concern; her thoughts are set on peace, in the Trinity. So while her loved one enjoys the blessed peace of the Trinity, she is not concerned about her sins or the sins of others. She is displeased by sin, since God is displeased by it, but sin cannot alter the peace in which God dwells, so it cannot disturb the peace of this soul. Of course she would help any of her fellow Christians if the opportunity arose, but her thoughts are so set on the things of God that she cannot be upset by anything concerning the transient doings of creatures: the goodness of God is beyond anything we can realize.

Giving nature all she asks

Such a soul can be said to give nature all she asks, willingly and ungrudgingly, because the spirit of possessiveness is dead in it, and the law of Christ – and his gifts, which are above the law – enshrined in its heart.

Love: That's right: this soul does not attach such importance to temporal things that it would worry her to have them denied her. So why be bothered about giving nature her due? But you must understand that I am talking about nature so well ordered by her closeness to divine love, to which this soul's will has been united, that she will ask nothing against God's will. The difficulty is to make sure that the ways of such souls are not taken as the ways of normal people; this is a risk one takes in describing them openly.

Using nature's bounty

(Love continues:) The souls we are discussing have such divinity in them that, even if they possessed nothing and knew they were going to live till judgment day, they would not worry about what they lacked, nor labour to supply it, unless it were a real natural necessity. And if they knew that others had greater need than they of something they possessed, they would not hesitate to give it to them, even if they thought the crops would fail for evermore. No one should doubt this: such is their nature, which shares some part of the divine nature.

Divine Justice: It is right that divine justice should be seen being fulfilled in these souls, and it would be lacking if they were seen to fail in charity. So why should they worry about taking what they need, and using what they are entitled to, when they need to? This would interfere with the peace in which they rest from such matters. Who worries about using light, heat, water and the fruits of the earth to sustain life? We take the four elements as we need them, as we do other things, without being troubled in conscience about doing so. So these souls can use the artefacts of the earth with a clear conscience, just as they use the earth on which they tread.

Impossible to describe God

Love: These souls are well grounded in good sense and sufficiently enlightened to be at peace. Yet even they can no more describe God than say where he is, or how good he is. Too much attempting to describe God to the first comer can easily lead to doubts.

The Soul: That is very true, and those who talk about God in this way have not felt the promptings of divine love which make them tend to be humble in these things, because these promptings really rid one of the habit of trying to describe God. Those who have felt them understand a lot and soon forget, so do not talk about such subtle matters.

Faith, Hope and Charity ask about these souls

Faith, Hope and Charity: Tell us where such perfect souls as you describe in this book are to be found, and what they are like, and what they do. Then we shall be able to calm those who would be dismayed or amazed by this book – as indeed the whole Church would be.

Faith: It's beyond me.

Love: Your 'lesser Church' that listens to the voice of reason might be amazed, but I don't think the 'greater Church' that is ruled by me would be.

  Why are you three asking where these souls are and what they are like and what they do? Surely you know that no one can find those whom God has made; yet you know where they are, because you three are always with them. You know what they are, too; but neither you nor they – nor even our holy mother the Church – knows what they are like or can describe their value or worth.

Reason: Oh, for God's sake, who does know then?

Love: Only God, who made them and ransomed them. It can often happen that they will be fulfilled, humbled and forgotten by his love.

Why should the Church be surprised that these holy souls are in control of the virtues? Why shouldn't they be? Surely the virtues were made, codified and ordained for souls, rather than the other way round? Surely the virtues must serve such souls, and the souls serve God, receiving from him the extraordinary gifts he witholds from those who are still bound up in will and desires? So those who want these gifts must forsake will and desire, or they cannot receive them.

Why does the Church not recognize these royal souls, these brides of Christ? The Church cannot recognize them without entering into their souls, and there is no room in their souls for anything made, but only for God, who made them. So only God who is in them can recognize them.

Reason: Please don't be angry with me, Love, if I ask one more question. If you don't answer it, I shall go on worrying about your saying that only God, who made them, can know these souls. My question is this: you say that only God who is in them can recognize them. And you said earlier that no one could find them except those guided by true love, but that these could find them and tell the truth about them. So it would seem that those that are like them can recognize them, if they happen to be in the same place?

Love: That is right: others like them, who happen to be in the same place, can know them by their habits, but mostly by the gifts given them, which are extraordinary.

Reason: Extraordinary! I'll say they are, and you're contradicting yourself in the most extraordinary way!

Love: Really, Reason, you must know that the same word can have different meanings. When I say that others like them can 'know' them by their habits, I mean recognize them, not fully know them as souls, in all their dignity and worth. This only the Lord God who made them can do.

CHAPTER THREE

From the virtues to freedom

The soul and the virtues

Reason: There is still another question that puzzles me, Love: in one place you say that this soul has no further need of the virtues, and in another that the virtues are always a part of this soul, more so than of any other. It seems to me that there is a contradiction here, and I fail to understand it.

Love: What this means is that the soul has moved beyond the virtues as far as trying to practise them is concerned, but the virtues have not departed from the soul; these are always there, but now it is they who are obedient to her. So she has taken leave of them, but they are always with her.

Let me give you an example: If a man has a servant, the servant can be said to be *with* the master, but you wouldn't describe the master as being *with* the servant. But if it so happened that the servant earned so much, and learned so much from his master that he ended up richer and wiser than the master, and was generally held in higher esteem, then the tables would be turned, and the master would recognize that the servant had taken over from him, and would stay on and serve him.

So with this soul and the virtues. At first she strove with might and main to do everything her mistress, reason, told her; and reason always told her to do everything the virtues required, without argument, to the death if need be. So reason and the virtues were the soul's mistresses, and the soul obeyed them in all things. But then the soul learned so much from the virtues that she rose above them, being capable of learning all that the virtues can teach and a whole lot more. This is because such a soul has the mistress of all the virtues in her: divine love, which has led her to God, so that she is no longer 'with' herself, nor 'with' the virtues.

Reason (still seeking to learn through asking): Who is she with, then?

Love: She is not with anyone, Reason, but 'by' my will, wholly attuned to me.

Reason: And who are you? Are you not a virtue like the rest of us, but rather higher than us?

Love: I am God, because love is God and God is love; this soul is God through love, and I am God by divine nature. By love's right, my beloved soul is taught and led by me with no labour on her part, because she is completely attuned to me. This is where her upbringing has led her. She has become the high-flying eagle, soaring above the other birds on the pinions of true love, seeing the bright beauty of the sun clearer than the others, and feeding on its warmth and light. And then she can say to her wretched nature, who was once her mistress: 'Mother nature, I take my leave of you, since I am held up by love, and held safe.'

Then there is nothing that she need fear, no comfort she needs, no hurt that can diminish her. Her generosity makes her a friend to all, in perfect charity, and she has no need to ask anything of anyone, because of the perfect goodness with which God has filled her. She can be modest without being dull, and happy without being wanton, because God has made his name holy in her, and the Blessed Trinity has made its dwelling in her.

The two props of the soul

Love: This soul set free has two props to lean on, one on her right and one on her left. With these she stands firm, like a castle set on a hill, or surrounded by a moat. One prop is keeping the gifts she has received, the true knowledge of her own poverty. This is the one on her left, and a great comfort it is to her. The other is the special knowledge of God to which she clings. With the two, she can live at peace, fearing no enemies on her left or her right.

She is, however, ashamed of her poverty, which she knows, and which seems to her a humiliation in the eyes of the world, as in her own. Also, she is drunk on her knowledge of the divine goodness, not that part of it she has known, but that part she has not known and never can know. So she is not drunk on what she has drunk, but on what she has not drunk and never will be able to.

Reason: That's a strange way to get drunk – on what

you haven't drunk and never will, I must say. If I understand what you are saying, it would be better for this soul to drink from the barrel of her loved one's goodness, as he does, than from what she has not drunk and never will, as he drinks from the divine tap in the same barrel.

Love: She can do this without actually drinking from it, in the sense that her love *must* share this tap, since there is no distinction between his nature and the divine nature, and so though she has not drunk from it, yet its 'must' has made her drunk. There may be many taps to a barrel, but the clearest and the strongest wine must come out of the one at the top, from which no one may drink except the Trinity. And it is the wine from this tap, though she does not actually drink from it, that makes the humbled soul drunk – well and truly drunk, on what she never drank!

The Church: Which just goes to show how carefully these high–flying souls have to watch themselves!

The Freedom enjoyed by these souls

Love: These souls keep a watch on their mind, understanding and will through their humility and discernment, which come from their appreciation of the things of God, and this keeps them free, because of their love of God.

Reason: Please explain, Love, how these souls find perfect freedom in their love of God.

Love: Through having no desires, nor allowing their feelings to be set on any object: those who do are far from enjoying the peace of true freedom. If their feelings are set on people, very few of these will allow them peace. These souls do nothing contrary to their inner impulses and so live at peace in love.

Once they have attained to this state, they have no other desires left; illumined by the rays of the sun of God's love, nothing can touch the purity of their hearts. Through knowing the greater − without consciously 'knowing' it − they are free from any craving for lesser things, nor can these ever give them satisfaction. They have a perfect unity of purpose, from which nothing can deflect them. Just as the sun gets its light from God and shines on all without its rays being sullied, so these souls get their being from God and nothing they see or hear can sully their brightness.

Reason: Does this mean that such souls feel no joy in anything in themselves, or outside them?

Love: No, they do not, because their nature is mortified and their spirit dead; they have died to will and live in a state of death according to the divine will. But mark carefully what this means: if a thing is on fire it is not cold; if someone drinks, he is no longer thirsty. These souls are so consumed in the fire of love that they cannot feel the flames, being fire themselves, aflame with pure love. This fire of love is all love, taking nothing from the will. If it took from the will it would be sensing God through something outside itself, through conscious effort, and this would add an impure substance to the fire. If you look to something outside yourself for an increase in love, you will see shadows in the flickering flames. But if you burn with the pure fire of love, without looking for anything outside to add to it, you will see things clearly as they are. There is then nothing in the soul to interfere with her clarity of vision, since she is at peace with herself through her humility, completely open to the impulses of charity, and united to God through the action of his perfect love.

She longer loves anything about God, however good, except for God's sake and because God wishes it. So she loves God in everything and everything for God's sake, and this makes her whole in the pure love of God's love. Then she sees so clearly that she sees God in her, not herself in God.

Meditation is better than consolations

Let me show you now, noble readers, what I mean through a meditation on the pure love that does not come through the senses, the love that is given to souls who do not desire any of the gifts of love, known as consolations of the soul, which bring a feeling of sweetness to prayer. Such feelings, and other practices, do not teach the soul; only love does this, and those who seek divine comforts in the shape of these consolations are debasing the currency of pure love.

Meditating on true love has only one aim: to love truly, without desire for any reward. The soul can only do this once she is stripped of all self-interest, because she must not look for any of the consolations that come from too much wanting. If she concentrates on herself, furthermore, she cannot pay full attention to what God is doing in her, or will God's will alone. This she must do, because if you start willing God to do your will and bring you his consolations, then you are not trusting in his goodness alone, but in the rich rewards he can give you.

The Soul: Quite right. Those who love truly seek only to give, not to take or ask anything for themselves. If they try to do both, one aim diminishes the other, so true love can only have one aim, and that is to love perfectly. The lover can have no doubt that her Beloved will always do what is best, and she seeks to do the same, and to will only that the will of God be done in her at all times.

Love: That is really all there is to it. The lover cannot will through her own will, since this is no longer 'in' her, but set in her Beloved, not through her own doing, but through the Trinity working in her.

In love's union, the soul is joy

Then she swims in a sea of joy, not feeling joy, but being joy; she drowns in this sea, enveloped in the joy that has made her joy. Like fire and flame, the will of the lover and the will of the Beloved are united, as the soul is totally drawn into the Beloved.

The Soul: Oh, the sweetness and truth and purity of this divine love! The joy of this union, in which I have become what I love more than myself! Even though I can love only feebly, Love has taken over my whole being, and I have become Love, my only love.

The soul cannot disturb her own peace: an example

Reason: Can you now explain, Love, what you meant by saying that this soul does nothing contrary to inner impulses and so cannot resist the demands of peace within her?

Love: Yes, it means that whatever happens, she does nothing contrary to the inner peace of her spirit. In this she is like an innocent babe, and this soul is innocence itself. Let me give you an example. Take a perfectly innocent child: is there anything that can make it do something it doesn't want to do? No, it is at peace with its own desires.

Translator: Love's example of the baby that will not do anything it does not want to do is meant to show that nothing can disturb the peace of its spirit. So with the soul drawn to the love of God (which Love takes in this book as standing for all who are so drawn): the Holy Spirit so guides it that nothing can affect it except the stirrings of love or what leads to love. And its spirit is in control of its body, not allowing it to become attached to anything that might get in the way of this divine love or what leads to it. So it listens only for the Lord's guidance, knowing that any other will disturb its peace, which is against the commandment of love.

The soul finds God in all things, but he cannot be understood

Reason: Now, Love, you should summon this soul to listen to what you have to say to her about him who is all in all.

Love: She knows he is, because she finds him everywhere, and in all things. So all things are fruitful for her, because she finds nothing that is not God. Why do you want me to call her?

Reason: Because otherwise I think she will be shy and hide.

Love: Believe me when I tell you this, Reason: everything the soul has heard about God, and anything she may hear in the future, is nothing compared to the reality, which is beyond the power of the tongue to describe. But listen, Soul, to something that will increase your joy and your sorrow, and remind you of all the favours you have received: all creatures who have lived and are yet to live in the sight of your Beloved have known nothing of him and will know nothing – in truth, knowledge, love or understanding.

The Soul: What shall I do, then, Love? I am more certain of what you have just told me than of anything else. But now there is something I should like to tell you, if I may.

Love: Tell me what you want, dear Soul, and I shall listen.

69

The soul's lament, Love's comfort, and her true comfort

The Soul: Why, dear Love, do you suppose God made me, and ransomed me, only to give me so little, when he has so much to give? If I had so much to give, I would not give my lover so small a part of it, yet I am nothing and he is everything. As it is, I have given him all I have – body, heart and mind – and he knows that full well. If I had anything left to give him I would, but he has taken everything of value from me (which he gave me in the first place) and yet he withholds himself. For God's sake, Love, is this the way you work?

Love: Come now, sweet Soul, you know better than to lament like this! If you have given him everything, you have given him nothing except what was his before you gave it to him, so you see that is the best thing you could happen to you!

The Soul: Yes, Love, you're right. I see it now and cannot deny it.

Love: What, my dearest, do you expect from him? Didn't he make you? Would you have him give you something that is neither his to give nor yours to take? You must console yourself with the gifts that rightly belong to you as a creature of God.

The Soul: You did not tell me this when I first met you! You said that there can be no division of rank between a lover and her Beloved – but there is! One has everything and the other nothing by comparison.

If I could change this I would: if I had the power you have, I should love him for all you are worth.

Love: That's enough; calm yourself. Your will is pleasing to your Beloved, and he has sent me to tell you that if you love nothing except him, then he will love nothing except you. This is a great privilege, and should comfort you, take my word!

The Soul: It would indeed if it could be so. But the most precious thing I have is that nothing I love is enough for me; if it were, I should be failing in the little love I have. The only thing that is enough for me is that the one who loves me more than I do myself has this quality of being totally unknowable, except by himself. This is my comfort, since I love him more than I do myself; he is my Lord and my God, my all. The fact that he lacks nothing makes up for what I lack. He is all goodness, without fault, and this is the source of my peace and happiness, since it is him I love, not myself.

I used to rejoice when I heard creatures speak of him, but now Love has told me the truth, which is that nothing people say of him can be anything compared to what he is, and what he is cannot be said. The best thing I can hear of him is this: that my love is less than the least thing he can be compared to, so there can be no end to my love for him, and my love will always find new love in him. Now I know that creatures can tell me nothing of him, and I don't really find what Love said comforting; it is comfort enough that no one can tell me anything about my Beloved.

Discretion: These souls certainly know how to make their point!

The Soul: What I know is that Love teaches us how to, and she is the boss in this book!

Better for the soul to love what she cannot have than what she has

(The Soul continues:) As I have said before, I don't feel the lack of anything as long as my Beloved is everything, without beginning and without end. It is not that I love myself, nor even him and all his works, but that I love for his sake. So what do I lack? What he has – which I can't have – is more mine than what I have and what he gives me.

Reason: Prove it!

The Soul: Very well! The proof is that I love one of the infinite good things about him a hundred thousand times more than I love the gifts he has given me, or will give me. This means that I love what I cannot understand in him more than what I can. What he knows and I don't is more mine than what I do, because most of what I treasure is where most of my love is. So I love the 'most part', which is what I can't know, more than I do the lesser part which I can. So, as love is my witness, I hold the greater part to be more mine than the lesser, because that is where most of my love is. And this is what gives me my peace of mind.

One thing I will say to you, Love, is that if it were in the power of any creature to give me the joy and glory

I get from God, I should always refuse it, rather than get it from anyone except direct from God himself. Indeed not, not even if the gift were everlasting, because I couldn't! I couldn't, because he has taken all my will to take, and that's the truth of the matter!

Be patient with me, Love, I beg you. I am abashed at my own temerity. How do I dare ask anything of him, who can no more be understood by his creatures than they can count the waves on the sea when a storm is blowing! Creatures are but flesh and blood, and cannot speak of the things of the spirit, so how can they speak of God? But anything is better than nothing, and so it is better to hear and read things about God than not to.

The soul's gifts and practices

(The Soul continues:) How, my Beloved, can I think straight when I consider all the gifts you have given me in your great goodness? You have given me the vision of the Blessed Trinity, Father, Son and Holy Spirit, to enjoy for evermore. If I can see this, I can know angels and souls too, and with this gift I can see everything that is less than God. Knowing this, I am so weighed down with what I know, all the time, that I have no time to practise anything other than the weight of this knowledge.

Translator: When the soul says that she has no time for other practices than the weight of this knowledge, she must mean during the time that she is engaged in this practice, because every practice has a time span, and the soul cannot really be continually engaged in just one. The workings of love and other dispositions suggest one practice followed by another. What she means is that such practices become habitual, and so she uses terms like 'all the time'. There are other terms in this book which need to be understood in the same way, not literally.

CHAPTER FOUR

The way to the union of love

The visions the soul has had

The Soul: Lord, if I had nothing else at which to marvel than this, that you have given me a vision of the Trinity and of the angels and holy souls that you denied to your Son made man, it would be more than enough! No human body is allowed to see the angels and holy souls, let alone the vision of the Trinity which you have granted me for evermore. Love, this knowledge frightens me! What shall I do with it?

Love: I shall tell you, but then don't ask me any more questions. If you properly realize your nothingness, you will do nothing, and this nothing will tell you everything. If you cannot properly appreciate your nothingness, the truth, then in truth you must do something, or risk losing what you have been given. If God has drawn you into his being, then you must remember what you were when he first made you, what you have been, are now and ever will be, except for those parts of you which are God in you.

The Soul: Lord, the only thing I know that can give me life is my sins for which you suffered death. I think – and rightly – that even if I were the only sinner the world has ever known, you would have ransomed my soul with your love on the Cross. So you have undergone all your sufferings just for me alone. All this, just for me! And so, Lord, now that you know that on my own I can do nothing, and am already so greatly in your debt, rid me of this burden, you who can do all things! Then I shall do your will in all things.

God's love for the soul has no beginning and no end

Love: Tell me what you are thinking, soul. It is not good to keep these things to yourself.

The Soul: It is this, Love: you told me that he who is in himself and of himself has no beginning and no end, and that he will never have anything outside me, nor I anything outside him.

Love: That is true, and I am the living proof of it.

The Soul: So if he will have nothing outside me without end, this means he never loved anything outside me. If he will be in me without end through love, then his love for me had no beginning either.

Reason: Watch what you're saying! Have you forgotten that not long ago you did not exist? Are you sure you know what you're saying?

The Soul: If I am wrong in this, then Love is in error too, since she taught me to believe it and say it. But you still don't see things clearly, Reason, and you cause a lot of trouble to those who try to live by you! So let me explain: if the Three Persons of the Trinity will love me without end, then they have loved me from the beginning. God loves me without end out of his goodness; he has known from the beginning in his wisdom that he would make me through his power. As God had no beginning, so there was no beginning to his knowledge that he would make me to have no end, nor to the love his goodness felt for the work he knew he would do in me, through his power.

Love: Quite so: as he is love, he has never withheld love and does not do so now.

Reason: Since Love guides you and speaks for you, I can argue with you no longer, but promise to obey you in all things, since this is Love's will.

The Soul: The tables are well turned – as they should be, because my Beloved does not want me to remain in your service. Once a lover has learned from him, she is free from you and other masters.

Love: That's quite right, dear Soul. Well put!

Reason: Just because Love lets you, you think you can say and do just as you please...

The Soul: Reason, you still don't understand! Why shouldn't Love let me? What I do is Love, my Beloved, doing it in me. Are you still surprised that he should want what I want? He has to, since I have no will except what he wants in me. This is why I live at peace, and there is perfect harmony between him and me.

How, sweet Lord, can I enjoy this peace, when you know how I have wasted my time? But of course I can, because your chivalry and nobility would not allow you to enjoy peace without my having it too! So as I find peace in everything I do, I know that you have rid me of the burden of my sin; however much I may have sinned, your peace lives in me. No one in this world, my sweet Lord, can know my sins in all their hideous number, but you alone. Those who are in heaven know them, but turn their knowledge to my glory, not my confusion, because in these sins that have offended you, your great mercy is shown and your endless forgiveness felt.

Love: And because of this forgiveness, this soul can be at peace with her conscience, whatever she does or fails to do.

The Soul: Lord, let me have a perfect will to do your will, because this is perfect charity.

Love: And whoever has perfect charity, need have no prickings of conscience, which indicate a failing of that perfect charity for which the soul was made.

The soul speaks through love

The Soul: Oh Lord, what have I been saying about you?

Love: Think back and see if you can work it out.

The Soul: You taught it to me, Love, and it went like this: Nothing is such that nothing must be nothing. So I must recognize what I have been saying as less than nothing. But what I say is said from divine knowledge, that is by you, Love. Your kindness, my gain: you get the glory, we get the merit – not those who read this book!

Oh Lord, you whom I love first and last, you suffer more willingly and patiently than any creature can say, from your great mercy, and despite my innumerable faults. I have wasted the idle moments I have spent withdrawn from giving you love and thanks and praise, and time lost in this way can never be recovered. I have often fallen this way, into deep darkness where the gifts of your grace that love has described for us are not to be found. And all that Love has said, through me, is but empty talk compared to the reality of your grace.

Reason: I was never so glad to hear anything. Now I understand perfectly that only you, Love, have the gift to make things clear.

Love: Indeed, this gift is given by none other than the Holy Spirit himself.

Reason: In that case, perhaps I do not understand it, but it seems to me that all this soul says and does is so well said and done that I want nothing more than to become her servant.

Love: If you really feel that, it's the best thing that could happen to you!

The example of the soul, and an example of moderation

Reason: What can I do now for those I have to look after, if this soul's outward example is going to be hidden from us?

Love: Is there any other example possible?

Reason: Not for those who can see clearly, or for those who are chosen to be perfect in this way, but there are not many of those on this earth, I'll be bound.

Love: What do you mean by example?

Reason: By example I mean a life of unremitting virtue, following your counsels and those of moderation, and the example of our Lord Jesus Christ.

Love: What you say about virtues and counsels is of little concern to this soul; she is above such things, since love has led her into union with him, and is at work in her, so that she has become love. And there is no moderation in love. We should be moderate in all things, except in love. Let me give you an example: it is like a landowner collecting rents by law; he does not owe his tenants rent, but they owe him rent. So all things owe me rent: the virtues can be counselled by reason and directed by moderation, but only those that are drawn and led upwards by love owe nothing but love. They have therefore paid love's due, as she has theirs.

The wise and the humble

I say that this soul is the wisest of my chosen ones, but

small minds cannot see this and cannot appreciate her worth.

Reason: Who do you call wise, Love?

Love: Those who are steeped in humility. They are right in everything they do, yet convinced of being always wrong. They see themselves as the worst of sinners, and this soul has long regarded herself as the servant of sin, lowest of the low, the least of all creatures. In this way, she has reduced herself to nothingness, and sees herself as less than nothing. Yet she has heard tell that the last shall be first, and that the meek will inherit the earth, and so she places all her trust and hope in the goodness of God, not in anything that she might do. The hidden worth of his goodness working alone in her has so deadened her, that she is immune to all inner and outer feelings. She can do no more 'works', either for God or for herself. She can no longer concentrate in her prayer; no longer deliberately look for God, or find him within her, or guide herself.

Where the soul is, what she knows and wants

Love: This soul is not *with* herself, and so is not responsible for her actions. The one in whom she is has taken on responsibility for her, to her great benefit.

Dread: If she is not with herself, where is she?

Love: Where she loves – without knowing it and so untroubled in her conscience. No inner voice guides her, because those who are guided by their conscience are conscious of themselves and so *with* themselves. Such souls have died of love and are no longer conscious of themselves, so they neither desire heaven nor reject hell, whatever they are told about the delights of the one and the torments of the other.

The Church: What, in heaven's name, do they want then?

Love: What they have become through knowing.

The Church: And what might that be? Holy Spirit, tell us, because we can't find the answer in our manuals, and so our reason cannot grasp what Love is saying. And she has made us feel so ignorant that that we can't argue against her!

The Holy Spirit: Oh you Church! So you want to know what this soul knows and what she wants? I'll tell you: she knows just one thing, and that is nothing; she wants just one thing: nothing. Through knowing nothing and wanting nothing, she has the greatest reward of fellowship without end in the Trinity, not through the divine nature, as that is impossible, but through the strength of love, which is irresistible.

Love: There, mother Church, now you know why this soul has everything.

The Holy Spirit: Yes, indeed, everything I have received from the Father and the Son, who know that she has everything I have, which is all that they have. So this soul has all the riches the Trinity can give living in her.

The Church (to the Holy Spirit): In that case, the Trinity must make its home with her and live there.

The Holy Spirit: That's right: the Trinity can live in her to the extent that she is dead to the world, and the world to her.

The Church: Oh Holy Spirit, true God indeed!

Love: You ought to be called 'the lesser Church' and such souls 'the greater Church', because it is they who support and teach and feed the whole Church – not just they, but the Trinity working through them. So, lesser Church, what can you say about such souls, who are so far above you – you who still follow the dictates of Reason in everything?

The lesser Church: We would say that these souls are a higher form of life than we are, since Love lives in them, whereas we only have Reason living in us. They are guided by love, and we by reason. But don't hold this against us, and remember that we praise such souls in our manuals!

The soul receives everything by giving everything

Reason: Now, Love, could you please speak a bit more clearly about these gifts that the Holy Spirit gives to such souls out of sheer goodness, so that some of us will have a chance of understanding such high matters?

Love: Oh Reason, you are still stupid and blind – you and those who follow you. None so blind as those who will not see, they say, and that's what you seem like to me.

The Holy Spirit: What I said was that I shall give this soul all I have already given her. All we have in the Trinity, in our knowledge of wisdom that had no beginning, has been promised to her out of our goodness. There is a good reason why we do not hold anything we have back from such souls: this soul has given us everything of value in her, and so you could say that she has given us what we have given her, since the proverb rightly says that the word can be taken for the deed.

If this soul possessed what we do, she would willingly have given it to us, just for the sake of doing our will, without wishing for any reward on earth or in heaven.

We possess all that we have by virtue of our divine nature, and *she* has given all she possesses by way of a love token; if there is to be justice in love's game, we must give her all that we possess in return. What we possess is ours by divine nature, and hers through love's justice.

The Church: We now understand and so believe the gifts you generously give in return for love. Love must always be the reward for love.

The soul languishing for love

Love: This soul's memory, understanding and will are of little account to her, since her whole being is fixed in God. God gives her being without her knowing or feeling or willing her being. All she knows is God working in her, and she languishes for love of him.

Reason: What does a soul languishing for love do?

Love: She fights vice by seeking virtue. In the end she will languish to the point of dying of love. She will then have bid farewell to the world, and the world to her; she will have taken refuge in God, where the vices cannot find her. In God she will know such contentment that neither the world nor the flesh nor the devil will miss her, since they will not be able to find her in her works. Created things no longer mean anything to her, and she lives at peace. So she can live in the world without a troubled conscience, and without will, since she has handed her will over completely to God's will, and wills nothing except that his will be done in the full measure of his goodness.

The Soul: You speak the truth, Love: I miss nothing in this world since I have no will. Only those who have humbled their will can know peace. By dying to will, I live in God.

Those who want nothing have no will, and this soul has abandoned her will so as to want nothing but the will of God, to whom she has handed over her will. So she lives in the freedom of perfect charity, and if anyone asked her what she wanted, she could only reply: 'Nothing!'

How the soul learns her nothingness and so believes in 'the greater'

The souls this book speaks of cannot learn their nothingness by anything in themselves, since they

85

have abandoned even the degree of knowing needed to learn this; such knowledge can only come to them by their belief in 'the greater'. Men can know nothing of God, even if they know as much as the souls of the blessed in heaven, which might be called a tiny part of God. This would tell them nothing of his power or his wisdom or his goodness; they would not know the smallest part in comparison to what he knows of himself. Or, to put it another way, all that has been said about him is nothing in relation to what he knows about himself. The tiniest bit of his goodness is so great that our greatest imaginings of goodness are nothing compared to the smallest part of the greatness of his goodness, let alone to all of him.

The Soul: Oh, then, Lord God, if I believe this, what am I to do?

God: You do nothing, but let me work in you. If you know you are nothing and believe in me, then you can do nothing. If you see your nothingness in relation to the greatness of me, then you are free and lack nothing, because there is nothing you can want.

So the soul knows 'the greater' only through not seeing her 'nothingness-in-God', but only his everything.

Reason: Heavens above! Can you really talk about 'nothingness' in God?

The Soul: Yes, if God wants me to. My will is God-given, but it is nothing compared to the tiniest spark of one part of his great goodness, as he knows it and we cannot. Think, then, how great his All must be, if this is true of the tiniest part! But only love can even think this, and that is enough for me.

Love: Now you see how the soul has come to believe in 'the greater'. She learns her nothingness by realizing that neither she nor anyone else has any conception of her faults compared to the knowledge God has of them.

The peace and freedom of the soul who wants nothing

(Love continues:) She has not kept any part of her will back in her; she wills nothing and knows she knows nothing and is therefore calm and at peace. What the Gospel says: 'If your eye is clear, then your whole body is lit up' (Mt. 6:22) can be said of her. She is not worried by what the Son suffered for her, because all her intentions are good, and any judgment she makes is made in charity. She lives always at peace because she carries this peace around with her, and so is at home and happy anywhere. She carries this peace through her life's work, which is done in perfect charity, so she is free in all things.

Being free, she wants nothing; anyone who has inner desires is not free, however good these desires are, because he is so much a slave to himself that he wants God to do his will, for his own glory. Those who want only God's will want nothing for themselves, except to carry out God's will for themselves and for others. But those who operate through their own wills leave no space for God.

87

The Soul: This is because they refuse to give themselves up to God's will, but they ought to learn to do so, or they will lose whatever their will may have gained for them.

Love: They are still slaves, though they think they are free, and so are happy with their lot.

The Soul: In fact they're so pleased with themselves that they can't see any better way and so they can never find one, but have to remain shut up inside their own wills. They will never find true happiness, because their wills will make them slaves as long as they remain within them. Their slavery comes from doing all they do out of reason and fear, whereas real freedom can only come from doing things out of faith and love. Then you neither fear anything fearful, nor desire anything pleasurable.

Love: Having no will of her own, this soul does not worry about what God may do, but only about doing his will in all things. She cares neither for heaven nor hell, nor for anything on earth. She neither desires nor refuses anything we can speak of.

The lesser Church (still relying on rational learning): For God's sake, then what does she want?

Love: Nothing; she wants nothing. This seems to some people, who put their trust in good works, to be neglecting endless opportunities for doing good.

The Soul: Such people are blind; they can't see the wood for the trees.

Love: That's right! Just as God's work is above man's work, so wanting nothing for God's sake is a better thing than wanting to do good for God's sake. If their determination to do good led them to perform miracles and be martyred every day, this would still not stand comparison with abandoning their wills to God. No, even being caught up to heaven with St Paul and seeing the vision of the Trinity itself is nothing, if it comes about from willing it. Enough of that!

The union of love

The soul is here cast in the mould of God, imprinted with his image as sealing-wax takes the image from the seal, and so can say:

The Soul: Though God's love for me is shown in the sufferings of his Son, this love is not against his will. Taking on human flesh and blood and dying for all humankind showed his goodness and was an expression of his divine will. Even if all those created with God's fore-knowledge were to be damned for all eternity, his love for me could not be against his will. The ransom paid by Jesus does not mean that all are saved. How do I know this?

Doesn't everyone know it to be true?

But you had better tell us yourself, Love!

God the Father: The one who needs telling is my eldest daughter, who has moved out of my ken, so that my Holy Spirit of love can teach her the secrets of my Son, which she has taught to this soul.

Love: This soul must be like God, as she has been

drawn into him and taken on his form, given to her from eternity by the one who has always loved her.

The Soul: He alone has made me no one, and this nothingness of being no one has placed me below nothingness itself; yet knowing my nothingness I have everything and between nothingness and everything there is no room for prayer, so I no longer pray.

The Church (the lesser, book-learning one): So what do you do, then? Tell us that.

The Soul: I live in peace, in the generosity of God's goodness alone, with no desires even for all the treasures he has in him. The sole purpose of my being is to empty myself of will. This sets me apart from myself, on my own and free. If I start willing things, I will be forced back into myself and lose my freedom, but as long as I will nothing and can take leave of my will, then I am supported by my freedom and need nothing else.

Love: Oh dearest soul, my sweet, you have said farewell to all outward forms of devotion, and in doing so refrain from their practice. Being made nothing, you have no life in which you can practise them, but swoon and die for love. Your love, my love, is all in him as he has made his secret dwelling-place in you. Your face is turned towards the sun of his love; you dwell in the house of his love, where none but those of your pure stock may enter; you bathe in the flood waters of God's love.

It is not by attempting to reach knowledge of God that the soul attains to these states. No understanding, however enlightened, can produce God's love. No, this soul beloved of God is clothed in the 'greater part' of God's love for her, which surpasses all. This soul is arrayed in the trappings of the all–surpassing peace in which she lives now, always has, and always will. She lives outside herself; just as ore heated in a furnace loses its elements in the stronger iron it becomes, so this soul loses her being in the 'greater part', which is heavenly peace, for which she has no dues to pay. She lives in the gentle land of surpassing peace, where nothing can disturb her – nothing created nor even commanded by God.

Reason: What is she concerned with, then?

Love: With praise of God, which is not made and never has been. Apart from this, she needs neither comfort nor concern.

The Soul: And so with God's praise I lack nothing and live at peace, without taking thought for other matters. This peace is the greatest of his gifts to me; through it I have but one being, one will, one love and one purpose. This is what the union of two natures in love has the power to give.

The need to be dead to the world

Love: This soul lets the dead bury their dead and leaves the damaged to practise virtue. And so she is concerned with none of the things of this world. The 'greater' teaches her her nothingness, and this teaches her how infinitely good and just God is. So she can look into the depths from the depths and up to the heights from the heights, see everything and nothing, as long as the two are united in her vision.

Reason: So, soul: you are in the depths and yet know the heights of perfection. These are obscure images love is using; the likes of you may understand them, but please try to tell the rest of us what they mean.

The Soul: Reason! It's true what they say: you have ears and do not hear! What Love says can only be said in condensed images, but you have dragged out the length of this book with your questions! If you and your insect-brained followers can't follow, this is because only those who are schooled in true love can understand what this book is teaching. If you want to understand it correctly, you need to be dead to the world, for otherwise you will not have the life of the Spirit in you.

PART TWO

The dialogue continues, mainly on the subject of the different stages reached by the soul

CHAPTER FIVE

The dark night

Perished souls

Reason: Now tell us how we must die to the world if we are to understand this book properly. It's not so much me or my followers who need to know, but those who have deserted me!

Love: There are three ways of dying to the world, and I will explain them to you in the course of this chapter, but I think you will find it hard enough to understand the first two, let alone the third, which I will come to later.

For a start, let me tell you about two ways of seeking perfection: a life of virtue, and a life of the spirit.

Those who practise the first mortify their bodies through continual good works, in which they take so much pleasure that they cannot believe there is a better way of life. They bolster themselves up with a continual barrage of prayers and good intentions. But because they cannot see the better way, they are blind and they perish for lack of spirit. They are called kings, but in a kingdom of the blind; those who can see call them rather slaves. For a crow, the prettiest bird in the wood is another crow, and this is how they see themselves. They live in a continual state of desire, and cannot believe that there is a better state to be in. And so they are held back from the life of the spirit, and perish on the way.

Virtues: Heavens above! What are you saying, Love? That all those who live according to us will perish? That's not what our textbooks say! We know that Christians who fail to follow us will perish, but we hope those who are taught by desire to follow us will not. We really cannot think you mean this!

Love: Of course you're right. It's a matter of knowing how to understand what I say. Therein lies the mystery of love.

Virtues: We'll have to take that on faith, since it's not in our nature to understand such mysteries. So please excuse us: we'll believe you according to the understanding we possess, since you have made us the servants of such souls.

The Soul: That's a fair admission you have made. Anyone who serves a poor master for a long time will have a poor reward, and this applies to those who serve the virtues, who cannot understand true love, as they have just admitted in the hearing of you all!

How can a virtue teach something it has never possessed, and never can? Now you know why those who desire to lead a life of virtue perish on the way.

Damaged souls: how they differ from perished ones

The damaged also seek their reward in this world, but they are wiser than those we have called 'perished'. So let Love tell us how these also seek the virtues, but in a more spiritual way, and what is better about them.

Love: Because they have a mind, and a very good mind, to seek out what we call the best, which the perished cannot aspire to.

Translator: The author is not using 'perished' in the sense of 'lost' souls, i.e., those that are damned. He means, as Love explains, those who rely on their own works, which they see as the best there is, and so cannot aspire to the higher things of the spirit. By following the lower way, they lose sight of the higher. Think of the two as goods in a shop: if they are 'perished', they are in a worse condition than if they are 'damaged'.

(Love continues): They see that there is a better way than the one they are following, but know that their understanding cannot reach it. Knowing this, they see themselves as 'damaged' in their understanding, and so they are, compared to the perfect understanding of the free soul. Compared to her, they are enslaved by their continuing desire to know the right way. But because they are like the 'little ones' and have the humility to ask the way, they may come to freedom through divine enlightenment.

Reason: Little? Can you yeally call them little ones?

The Holy Spirit: Yes, as long as they continue to seek guidance from knowledge or love, or do things from love or knowledge or desire, because no wise man prays without good reason, or worries about what he cannot have. So those who ask often are little, and those who ask nothing are great, but all men are like reeds swaying in the wind, and less than nothing compared to the highest state of not-willing, where those free souls who have reached this state ask nothing and desire nothing except to give themselves in perfect love.

Introducing the concept of the 'dark night'

Love: Yes, they give everything that God values. They are neither perished nor damaged.

Such a soul has reached the fifth stage on her way – tranquility – and wants for nothing. From there she is sometimes snatched up to the sixth stage – entering light – which lasts but a moment, open and shut, and is brought about by the Beloved. No one can stay long at this stage, and no mortal being can describe it.

When this moment opens out, the soul shuts off and rests in the peace this stage brings, free and at ease, free of all encumbrances and of all created things, for as long as the peace of the moment lasts. When the light is shut off, the soul returns calmly to the fifth stage, without ever falling back to the fourth, which contains will, which the fifth does not. This call from the fifth to the sixth stage is a blinding flash from heaven, as soon over as begun, and the peace it brings is such as no one who has not experienced it can believe.

It is a marvel to the soul, the glory of heaven itself. It lasts only the time it takes to work in the soul, and no creature can stay long in this state, so noble and good it is. It is a heavenly food for the soul, but only those in whom desire is dead can enjoy it.

The three lives and deaths of the soul

(Love continues:) At first, this soul lived in the life of grace which is born from the death of mortifying sin. Then she lived in the life of the spirit, born from the death of mortifying her nature, and finally, in the life of glory, born from the death of mortifying her spirit. Once she has reached this life of glory, she always lives outside herself.

Reason: When does she live inside and when outside herself?

Love: She lives outside herself when she lives in nothingness: not in God, herself or her fellow-Christian, but in the nothingness brought about in her by this dark night. She cannot tell of its approach, nor of its going away. The nothingness it brings carries its own forgetting of the experience. If only one could understand how much a moment of this nothingness is worth – how rich one would be!

The first death – the death of sin

Love: Reason asked how many deaths the soul had to die before coming to this life of glory. There are three, of which the first is the death of sin. To this, the soul must die completely, retaining no sight, taste or smell of anything God's law forbids. People who die this death live in grace, which is sufficient for them to be saved: doing what God commands and abstaining from what he forbids.

You finer souls who have been made nothing and raised up by union with divine love, forgive me if I say something for the less advanced! I shall say more directly to you later. A contrast can often help understanding, in any case, just as white shows up better from having black placed next to it, and vice versa. Remember that it is a long road from the first stage of grace to the final stage of the life of glory, which the dark night gives. If you can understand this with the thoroughness of the sanguine disposition, and grasp it with the speed of the choleric, nature will be helping you on your way. And when the third element, righteousness, is added to these two sides to nature, then this combination produces a glad anticipation of glory. Which, I wonder, is the happier: the soul in this glad anticipation of the glory that attracts the soul and ennobles it by making it obey its nature, or the soul that is united to glory?

The Author: You are better able to say that than I am, Love, and your word is my command. I have tried my hardest to make it possible for those who read this book quickly to desire the experiences of love it describes, even if they have not come to them yet. And if some readers have already passed this stage and have got to that of not-willing and freedom from all things, then they should be careful who they tell how they understand this book.

Love: The life of glory, as I have said, is exceedingly difficult to understand. It is as far above the lower stages as the whole ocean is greater than a drop of water in it. The comparison even holds good for the first stage compared to the second and the second compared to the next: there can be no comparison between them. But still there is no stage among the first four so high that in it the soul is free from some form of bondage. It is only at the fifth stage that it is freed from all created things by charity, and the life of glory begins at the sixth, which is when the dark night gives a swift glimpse of glory, a glimmer God allows the soul of the glory that one day will be hers for ever. Then in his goodness he gives a glimpse of the seventh and final stage, to which the sixth gives access, but this glimpse is so swift that the person allowed it has no knowledge of being given it.

The Soul: What is this marvellous gift that I have been given without knowing that I was receiving it? When it was being given to me, I felt that I had become one with the gift itself, and if I had died at that moment, I would have had it for eternity.

What the dark night is, and the knowledge it gives to the soul

The Beloved: This night is nothing less than the Trinity itself, showing its inner being to the soul. The Trinity opens itself up to the soul and shows her its glory, known to itself alone. Then the soul that receives the gift of this vision of glory has God's own knowledge of God and of herself, and sees everything through God's sight. But the light of this divine knowledge takes all consciousness, of God, of herself and of all things, from her.

The Soul: This is so. When God wants me to know him, he takes ordinary knowledge away in this dark night, because there is no other way of knowing him.

When I am conscious of knowing myself, the dark night takes that knowledge away from me also, since otherwise I could not come to greater knowledge of myself.

The three deaths

Love: Now then, Reason, let me return to what I was talking about before. I had got as far as those who were dead to sin and so alive in the life of grace. They do just what God tells them to do, without being concerned for more. They seek honour in the world, but not excessively, not to the point of sin. They enjoy being rich, and hate being poor – particularly if they have been rich once and lost their money – but not excessively, not if it means going against God's will. They enjoy leisure, but are not slothful. They have died to sin and live the life of grace.

The Soul: These are negligible people, of little account on this earth, and of even less in heaven!

Reason: Watch your words! You shouldn't call anyone negligible when God will have them in his sight for all eternity.

The Soul: Yes, I can, there is no way of comparing their littleness with the greatness of those who have died the death of nature and live in the life of the spirit.

Reason: I appreciate that, and so do these people. They know me well, but won't listen to me: they say God has only advised them to do so, not commanded them, so they don't have to unless they want to! Which is hardly considerate of them ...

Jesus Christ: It certainly is not! They forget that whatever I did for them, I did to the utmost in my humanity, even to the death I suffered on the Cross.

The Soul: Dear Lord, don't trouble yourself on their account. These souls are so wrapped up in themselves that they forget you. Their small-mindedness is enough for them, and there is no room for you in it.

The Soul: They are the tradespeople of the spiritual life, its wage slaves, meddling with goods that the gentle folk of this life would not dirty their hands with. They are not admitted to the charmed circle of Love's close friends, where the next class are to be found. These are those who never forget Love's humiliations and sufferings, which they are constantly holding up to themselves as a mirror and example. These are the ones who have died the death of nature.

Love: These have everything they need to be saved, since they listen to the Gospel. They are much more considerate than the first lot, but still small in comparison with those who have died the death of the spirit and live in the life of glory, which no one can know without dying the death of the spirit.

Truth: These souls are the apples of God's eye, and nothing stands between them and God. They have gone beyond the pleasures of earthly love and the feelings of love for God, into the purity of divine love.

Love: This divine love brings them rest and peace and calm, but also flame and fire: it is Love who tells you this.

This love is the union of love, a pure flame burning without smoke, into which the soul can advance without fear, since her Beloved is at work in her.

These then, are the three deaths through which these souls come to the three lives.

CHAPTER SIX

The ways of contemplation

The power of the freedom of love

The free soul is stripped from her body, but clothed in the life of glory. Her spirit is stripped from her body so that it is not in her body, since her bodily sensuality has been removed by the power of God. So she goes naked into an unknown land, not remaining in her body, though she still gives it life. This is the power of the freedom of love.

Now her greatest joy is to have freed herself from the domain of reason and the other virtues, so bound up in being chosen by God that her discourse begins where theirs leaves off. This choice is beyond human power; the summons comes from the Holy Spirit, writing a mysterious text on the precious parchment of the soul, in words no human mouth can utter.

The unknown land

Reason: Tell us something about this unknown land into which the soul goes.

Love: It is where the soul is through him, with him and in him; where she receives no gifts except from him.

Truth: Then this land must be God the Father, since we know that he is the only person of the Trinity who has not received anything from any of the other persons.

Love: That's right, since God the Father has divine power in himself without having received power from any other person, and gives the Son what he has, so the Son receives it from the Father, and becomes equal to him. Now the Holy Spirit proceeds from the Father and the Son, one person in the Trinity, separate from the others, as the Son comes from the Father and the Holy Spirit comes from the Father and the Son. The free soul is taken up and united to the Trinity, so that she has no will but that of the Trinity, through the operation of the whole Trinity. And she is touched with a blinding light which transfixes her and nourishes her on the most high God.

The labour of following reason

The Soul: Oh, you small-minded, coarse people who follow the asinine course of reason! I am not going to descend to your petty level, but will tell you in my own language the secrets I have learned at God's secret court, where generosity rules, love commands and goodness provides. I am drawn to its beauty and calm, so can only desire to live in peace.

Reason: What do you think my followers do, then?

The Soul: I think they are confined in the temple of the law, and labour by the sweat of their brow to earn their bread. But I have become a temple of the spirit, redeemed in the precious blood of our Lord, and beyond these crude labours. They need reassurance, and Christ will not fail them, as his dying for them proved, and as the gospels – which refresh those who labour – witness.

Reason: And where do you get your refreshment? You don't seem to labour in your temple, except through the higher gifts of love and faith.

The Soul: No, I am freed from all labour, and I refresh myself in ways that are so far above yours that no comparison can be made between them. God chooses me in this way, but not in our time.

Translator: The soul says that her ways are not those of labour; they are so far above them that they cannot be compared, and this is of God's choosing, but not in our time. She refers to the times she is snatched up into union with God; this has nothing to do with our time, as human weakness cannot allow the soul to be taken away for more than a moment of our time. If the pull of sensuality is strong, then the soul can never be so taken away – this applies to heretics. Heretics are also prevented from attaining to this state through their natural intelligence: there is no way they can reach God.

All such sayings in this book have to be understood with this in mind. The book tries to show those who are disposed to subtle spiritual exercises the real way to reach an understanding of God, and so understand the heavenly conditions to which he alone can bring the soul.

In several places in this book, the 'free soul' rebukes

– in a way – those who concentrate on their spiritual development through outward forms of devotion, instead of looking deeper inside themselves, encouraging them to hold back sometimes and enjoy the peace of true love. As the Psalmist says: 'Pause a while and know that I am God' (Ps. 46:10), meaning: 'Take a rest from your outward labours sometimes, see the goodness of God and let him work in you'.

The soul also says she does not pray. This should not be taken to mean she never prays, but that in certain states she cannot pray in the normal way. Such souls are sometimes granted a vision of God's secret judgments and providence. At such times, their wills are so bound up with God's, through obedience, that they cannot pray for themselves or for other people. Even if in their prayers they might have prayed for other things, what they want most is God's will to be done. When they are turned in on themselves (in contemplation) they cannot pray, but their whole being is a prayer in God's sight. But at other times they pray normally, according to the rules of the Church, uniting their will always to the will of their Saviour. But when they are in the condition of glory this soul describes, they are incapable of physical activity. So the remarks about 'never labouring' must be taken as referring to these moments of rapture, which this book is about – though there is more to them than can be said in this book, as you can readily imagine.

I have said enough – at least till I feel I have to put in another word of explanation. I have tried to explain aspects that have caused confusion, though I know others could have done so much better. Excuse my ignorance, readers, and remedy my failings – and if anything I have said proves helpful, then let the honour be God's, the source of all goodness: 'Not to us, Lord, not to us, but to you alone is the honour due' (Ps. 115:1).

The Soul: Now, Reason, you want to know what ways I follow? Those of him who is so strong that he can never die, whose teaching cannot be put into words, shown by example or taught. He has known from eternity that I must believe in him without looking for any proof for my belief, since love seeks no reward. As love is its own reward, so he is proof enough for me; if I were to look for any other, I should not be believing in him.

Reason: I can see that there is one law for your sort and another for mine, and yours governs love and ours belief. So you are free to say what you like and regard us all as donkeys!

The Soul: If I call you donkeys it is because you look for God in creatures and in nature, striving to find him with your senses: heaven is not built in this way, and cannot be captured in words or writing. Benjamin has not yet been born in you, since Rachel still lives and she has to die in giving birth to Benjamin.* People

* Benjamin stands for contemplation, and Rachel for reason. The allegory was developed by Richard of St Victor, whose treatise on 'The Way to True Contemplation, or Benjamin' was translated into English by the author of *The Cloud of Unknowing*, and is included in *A Letter of Private Direction and other Treatises* in this series (*ed.*).

who look for God in hills and woods and valleys see him as bound by his sacraments and works, and are silent and miserable for not finding him. But those who find him everywhere, not just in forests or on mountain-tops, through uniting their will to his, have a happy and enjoyable life.

Reason: And where do you find him, noble soul?

The Soul: I find him above everything, one God in three persons. This is the God who is above everything, and this is where I find him, for I am what I am by the grace of God alone, and I am nothing apart from God in me. God is what is in me. The best there is is what is most loved, and that is what he is. If I alone am what is, then I am nothing, but nothing is, except God, and so I find nothing except God wherever I look, because there is nothing except him.

It is not the soul that lives in truth, which is God, but truth that lives in her and works out all his sayings in her.

Love: That's right. Others answer by trying to complicate the issue, but these stripped souls are forgetful and have no case to answer. And, as I have said earlier in this book, these souls do not labour on their own account, nor on God's nor on their fellow Christians'. God, who can do everything, does these works for them, if he wishes, and if he does not wish to, this is all the same to them. The enlightenment of divine knowledge does this for these souls, drawing them out of themselves into a state of uncaring divine peace, marked by a joyous drowning in love of the

Almighty, the jealous God who gives them the power of freedom in all things.

The Soul: He would indeed seem to be jealous, since he has taken me out of myself and placed me in a divine pleasure garden outside myself, where I am united with the other half of that union, God, who is divine and so gives me a divine existence.

Love: And when this soul is taken out of herself in this way, through God, with him and in him, she is unable to perform physical works of charity, and the same applies to all who reach this state.

The Soul: Mark Love's words carefully and under-stand them in the sense in which they are to be taken, which is not easy.

Love: Quite so: human work cannot be compared to God working in his creatures, for his creatures, out of his goodness.

Consequences of the wickedness of Lucifer and his followers

The Soul: What a long way the perished and the damaged are from the land of freedom and achieved peace where we dwell!

Love: The reason for this is that the perished and the damaged are still subject to their wills. Remember that when God made the angels, some were wicked because they chose to follow the evil designs of Lucifer, who wanted to have as his right what he could only have through God's grace. So from following their will in this, they fell from grace and are now in hell without hope of recovering the sight of God. So by choosing their will and using it to desire what they could not have, they lost their original vision of God. And now look what has become of them!

Truth: So why do we love our wills so much, when they can lead to this?

Love: Souls have wills when they still live the life of the spirit. As long as they remain at that stage, they will have wills.

Why talk about 'soul' rather than 'spirit'?

Reason: Why, Love, do you call your chosen one 'soul' rather than 'spirit', while you have just said that the damaged have wills because they are still in the life of the spirit. Surely 'spirit' is a worthier name than 'soul', which is only a little thing? This constantly surprises me.

Love: That's a good question, and raises an essential point. So listen carefully. Those who live in the life of grace, keeping the commandments and content with that, are called 'souls', not 'spirits'. The orders of angels have different names, but are still all known as 'angels'. The lowest order are just angels, while the highest are seraphim and also angels. Do you see what I mean? Those who only keep the commandments are 'souls' but not also 'spirits' because they do not live in the life of the spirit. The body and the will must be mortified before a soul can be all spirit; people come to 'spirit' when they take pleasure in poverty and hardship, but do not reach the 'death of the spirit' while they still retain something of their wills. The spirit will not die till it has shed the sensations of love and died to the will that gave it life. This is the true fulfilment of will through God's will, and the death that brings the free and perfect life in glory.

No one can attain to this perfect life except through loving me for what I want alone; otherwise the soul is *with* herself, not with me. But those I have taken as my lovers can no longer be with themselves: were they the greatest sinners in the world, or had they all the gifts enjoyed by the souls in paradise – with their wickedness and reward plain for all the people to see –, they would be neither ashamed nor proud, nor would they seek to justify themselves. To do so would be to be *with* and *for* themselves, not with and for me. Shame and honour in the world's eyes are all the same to them; they are content to let the Master blame or praise them as he wishes.

You were asking, Reason, why such souls are here called by the 'little' name of 'soul', not 'spirit'. I have called them this for short, as we normally know things by one name alone, but they could properly be called 'pure heavenly spirits of peace'. From the depths of the valley they can see the mountain they are to climb through the eyes of faith, where the All-powerful will unite them with the gifts of the Trinity, and nourish them with the peace of the glorious land where those who love God live. They are Maries of peace, with their eyes always fixed on the heights of peace brought to them by their Beloved, free of the cares that keep the Marthas of this world from the life of peace.

Reflections on our Lord's transfiguration

Those who understand according to nature know that when Jesus was transfigured on Mount Tabor, he had with him only three of his disciples, and he told them not to say anything of what they had seen till he had risen from the dead. But do they know why he took only three of his disciples with him?

The Soul: No, they know only the chaff of the reason, not the grain of it. But I know why: it was because only those who love him in a special way can see the brightness of his transfiguration. And taking them up on the mountain means that those who are still engrossed in temporal matters here below cannot see this divine brightness, because these matters are lower than God. And the reason he forbade them to speak about what they had seen was to prevent them from boasting.

Peace and freedom can only be achieved by openness to grace

(The Soul continues:) Understand the great and unending gift of love, which may make two into one in an instant. But there is one thing I must still say, not for those who have achieved peace, but for those who are still on the way. That is, that they must be ever on their guard, so that when love sends them anything, they are in a condition to accept it, not refuse it on any account.

Whenever love's message comes, they must never refuse to accept it. They must be careful that the virtues are not so much in control of them that they fail to recognize the call of love, who is the messenger of the Sovereign Lord. If they do, they will never reach the state of peace, but remain troubled and worried from lack of trust.

CHAPTER SEVEN

Advice to those on the way

Love rebukes those who refuse God's message

You who read this book must understand what it means, because a thing is only worthwhile to the degree that it is understood. What you need is what I wish for you, yet you have constantly refused to accept my messages. I have sent Thrones, Cherubim and Seraphim, to call you, enlighten you and embrace you, to show you my desires for you, but you have sent them all away. When I saw that you had done so, I decided to leave you to wander in the wilderness of your own knowledge, whereas if you had listened to my messengers, you would have had new life. But as long as you persist in living according to your own natures, you will always be burdened, whereas if you had listened to my messengers you would have been freed from your cares. Oh soul, can't you feel the weight of the cares you have taken on yourself?

The Soul: Yes indeed! My body is weak and my soul fearful, and I groan at the thought of the far-off freedom I am missing.

Love: What a lot of trouble to so little profit! And all because you would not listen to the lesson of perfection, which was to rid yourself of worldly cares while you still had time! But you would not listen to those I sent to teach you this, and those who do not listen to them will have troubles till they die.

Had they only wanted to, they could have been set free from all the cares and burdens they suffer, at so little profit to themselves, which make them so badly off compared to those who have been set free. And all they had to do was to give themselves to me when I would have taken them. They only had to listen to the Virtues whose task it is to show them the way, who told them what they had to do if I was to come and give them the freedom of my embrace. So instead of being with me, they are 'with' themselves, in the state I have described earlier. This is how the free souls see the others who are still in slavery, shown up to those who can see clearly like specks of dust in the sun's rays. When the sun is in the soul and its ray in the body, then the body is weak no more and the soul has no more fear. Christ is the Sun, and when he performed his miracles, he never healed the soul without the body, but always body and soul together, and he still does so now he is in heaven, but only to those who believe in him.

So belief and love are both needed, and then the soul will be free and strong, without cares or burdens, but faith is the first gift needed.

How the 'damaged' can reach the next stage of perfection

Love: I have told you how those who should have obeyed the call of my messengers and followed their

118

teaching, but have not, will live burdened for the rest of their lives, however hard they try through reason and good intentions to carry out the teaching of the apostles. Their approach is too deliberate and too complex to allow them to enjoy the simplicity of peace. They are not obeying the inner impulse to love but still trying to do everything by their own efforts.

The Soul: All you who seek perfection, be on your guard so that when the inner demands of your spirit summon you to the next highest stage – the one after that we have called 'damaged' or 'life of the spirit' – you will not refuse the summons.

Love: Yes, those who are at the first or second stages of the life of perfection must be on their guard to follow all the good impulses of their souls if they are to come to a higher stage: they are at present just servants preparing the house for the Lord to come and live in it; when he arrives, he will free the soul into the stage of wanting nothing, which can only come through giving everything, since those who give shall receive.

The Soul: So the 'damaged' must live in peace and follow the promptings of their spirit when it urges them to love, being careful not to become so wrapped up in conscious reasoning that they cannot hear the spirit when it prompts them. Then they will move on to the stage just below the perfect freedom we have been discussing. This is not to say that they should abandon pious practices and consideration for their fellows, any more than Christ did when he was on this earth to give us life. He felt pity and consideration for his fellows, but due consideration means seeing and loving in them the things that are most worth loving. So if you love temporal things, you cannot love spiritual ones; if you love with bodily love, you cannot love with divine love. If you love God as he is, you will not be conscious of the humanity of Christ – at least while you are possessed by divine love. While a soul still loves physical things, she cannot have God living in her or be united to him. How can these souls feel, for God does not change, and nor do they?

Translator: You will have to think carefully to understand what is meant here. When the soul says that she cannot feel things in herself, and does not change, she is referring to the moments when she is caught up in union with God. This is the highest type of union, where the soul is ravished by love and so bound and united to God that God and the soul become one being. As St Paul says: 'He who is united to the Lord becomes one spirit with him' (1 Cor. 6:17). So how can the soul feel things herself at this time, or change? Of course she cannot, because her whole being is fused into God's. This blessed state can only last a moment while we are still in this life, as the body cannot stand it for longer, but God can grant it often to those to whom he is pleased to give this great favour – glory and praise be to him for evermore.

Many obscure passages in this book have to be understood as referring to these moments of rapture. If you find them hard to understand at first, keep re-reading them and offer up your lack of understanding;

then the meaning will gradually become clear to you. (I know I said I wouldn't offer any more explanations, but I felt I had to here – and may have to again. God help us always to do his will in all we do.)

Free souls are never burdened

Love: When these souls have come to love God as he is, they are made conscious of their own nothingness – being nothing, having nothing, either from themselves, their fellow-Christians, or even from God himself. The soul is then so small she cannot see herself; all created things are so far from her she cannot feel them; God is so infinitely greater she cannot grasp him. Through this nothingness, she has the sureness of knowing nothing, being able to do nothing by herself, and willing nothing. And this nothingness brings her everything, which otherwise she would not have.

She is afloat on a sea of peace, drifting without any impulse from inside herself or any breeze from outside – both of which can undo peace, but not for her, because she is in full command and beyond interference or care. If she did anything through her outer senses, this would remain *outside* her, and if God did anything in her, this would be him working in her, for his own purpose, and so also *outside* her. What she does no more burdens her than what she does not do; she has no more being in herself, having given it all freely without asking 'why?'. She no longer feels doubt nor trust.

Reason: What does she feel, then?

Love: Absolute certainty, and total acceptance of the divine will; this is what makes her completely free.

The free soul lost in love

Being completely free, and in command on her sea of peace, the soul is nonetheless drowned and loses herself through God, with him and in him. She loses her identity, as does the water from a river – like the Ouse or the Meuse – when it flows into the sea. It has done its work and can relax in the arms of the sea, and the same is true of the soul. Her work is over and she can lose herself in what she has totally become: Love. Love is the bridegroom of her happiness enveloping her wholly in his love and making her part of that which is. This is a wonder to her and she has become a wonder. Love is her only delight and pleasure.

The soul now has no name but Union in Love. As the water that flows into the sea becomes sea, so does the soul become Love. Love and the soul are no longer two things but one. She is then ready for the next stage.

Reason: Can there be a next stage after this?

Love: Yes, once she has become totally free, she then falls into a trance of nothingness, and this is the next highest stage. Then she lives no longer in the life of grace, nor in the life of the spirit, but in the glorious life of divinity. God has conferred this special favour on her, and nothing except his goodness can now touch her.

May God grant you – those for whom Love has made this book, and for whom I have written it – to come to

this life of being in him where there can be no change!
But those who have not known this favour, and never
will, will never understand it, try as they will. What it
means is being in God without being oneself, since to
be in God is being. But here the race is to the swift,
and those who cannot swim in these waters will
drown, and may drag others down with them.

Reason: Well put! Those who still have burdens tend
to heap them on to other people's shoulders!

Charity and good works: Reason is shocked to death

Love: This soul is consumed in the flames of charity,
and her ashes blown into the sea. Generous in good
times, and even more so in bad, she is the essence of
nobility in all she does.

The Soul: Her way to God is no longer through
penances, nor the sacraments of the Church, nor
thoughts nor words nor deeds. She is not helped on
her way by creatures of this earth nor by those of
heaven. She is beyond justice, mercy, glory, the
knowledge and love of God, beyond praising his
name.

Reason: Good God! What are you saying now? What
am I or my followers supposed to make of this? I can't
find any way of excusing a claim like this!

The Soul: Your brood have legs and cannot walk,
hands and cannot work, mouths and cannot speak,
eyes and cannot see, ears and cannot hear, reason and

cannot think. Their bodies are lifeless and their minds dim. No wonder they are shocked!

Love: Yes, they must be amazed. They are far from the state in which these things can make sense to them. But those who live in the land of God have no trouble in understanding them.

The Soul: Think of it like this. If a king had a subject who had served him well, so well that he gave him a great gift which meant that he never had to work again for the rest of his life, would you blame the king for his generosity? No, why should anyone with any sense be shocked at this? My Beloved is the greatest king of all, and gives his great gifts freely to those he loves. So, those who are enlightened and fulfilled by the favour of his love have no further need of the consolations of this world. They can go direct to his peace.

Martha is troubled about many things; Mary is at peace. Martha is praiseworthy, but Mary more so. She has but one desire, and that brings her peace, whereas Martha has many concerns, and these cause conflict. So a free soul has only one desire. She hears what she cannot hear, exists where she cannot be, feels what she cannot feel. She holds on to this: he is with me, there is nothing I shall fear.

The Soul: With him, she is queen of virtues, daughter of the Godhead, sister of wisdom and bride of Love. Reason will wonder at such language, but he has reached his limit, whereas I was, am and shall be for evermore: love has no beginning or end, and is beyond understanding and I am pure love. How then can I ever end?

Reason: This is too much for me! I cannot bear it! My heart fails me and I am slain! (*Dies*)

The Soul: He should have died before. Now I can come freely into my own. The wound of love is the death of reason.

The soul's will fixed in the Trinity

Love: This soul has no need to perform mundane tasks, because she lives in freedom. Those who have been truly caught up and captured and completely taken over by love, have no heart for anything but love, even if they have to suffer love's pangs and torments for ever, even though their sufferings are as great as God is good. Those who doubt this have not loved truly.

Everything this soul has comes to her from the Trinity. Her will is so firmly fixed on the Trinity that she can no longer sin unless she can unfix it; there is nothing she can sin with, since without will no sin is possible, and her will is in the Trinity. So provided that she leaves her will where she has fixed it, in the Trinity who freely gave it to her in the first place, there can be no talk of sin in her. She has fixed her will wholly and freely in the Trinity, without pausing to ask 'Why?' not for her own sake, but because it is good to do so and because God wills it. She has not known constant peace till she has left her will fully in God in this way. In this state she is as if drunk, with no fear of anything that might happen to her, but if she still retains something of her will, then she should fear dangers, since she is not all at one, not being completely nothing. As long as she has a will to give or to withhold, she is divided in herself.

What those who are still in the life of the spirit must do

(Love continues:) I have this to say to those who are still in the life of the spirit: if I require it of them, they must follow the inner promptings of their desires in their quest for perfection through reason, whether they want to or not. If they do this, they can yet reach the state we have been discussing and be masters of themselves as well as of heaven and earth.

The Soul: To do this they must not set their hearts too anxiously on what they do and give and possess; if they do, then they have not reached this stage.

Love: I said that they have to look to their innermost desires; if they can forsake all their outer desires and turn to the inner life of the spirit, then they can come to this mastery.

The Soul: This is something that only God, who *is* this mastery in creatures, can see. But I can tell you what souls have to do before they reach God; they have to do the contrary of their inclination always to give way to the demands of the virtues, so that the spirit alone may dominate them without fear of contradiction.

Truth: I pity the poor body that has to suffer such a spirit!

The Soul: If the spirit is fervent enough, it can take away all pains of the body in an instant, provided that the inner spirit is worked on hard enough.

Love: What the body of those who are still in the life of the spirit has to learn is always to do the opposite of what it wants to do, the opposite of what pleases it most. Otherwise the soul will slip back from the life of the spirit. But once the soul has become completely free, the opposite is the case: then the soul has to do exactly what it pleases, or it will slip back from the life of peace. Once the soul has progressed from virtue to love and from love to nothingness, it has to do exactly what pleases it, or it will lose its peace and freedom. The soul is totally pure only when she has passed the threshold of doing the contrary of her desires and does what most pleases her. This is her crossing of the Red Sea, leaving her enemies drowned behind her. What pleases her then is my will for her, since she enjoys pure unity of will with God, in whom I have placed her. Having moved from grace to perfection, from the virtues to love, from love to nothingness and from nothingness to the enlightenment of God, who at this stage gives her his light so completely that she can no longer see either herself or him, then her will has become mine.

She can no longer see herself because if she could she would still be conscious of herself. God, who has known her from all eternity, sees his own goodness in her. In giving her his goodness, he has made her

127

mistress of her will, which is the gift of his goodness, and he cannot take this free will from her without her consent. Now he has her will just as he did before he made her mistress of it, without question. Now there is nothing except him and no one is loved except him, since no one exists except him.

This singles her out, makes her a soul set apart, and the all-ness and unique-ness of his being brings her to the highest stage of the life of perfection that any creature can reach in this life. There are five stages below this, and the seventh, the only one above it, is to be reached in paradise. This is the great goodness of God working in his creatures. The Holy Spirit blows where he will and works wonders.

The peace of this state: our Lady as example

The Soul: This wonderful gift of love, led and enlightened by God himself, is an enduring peace: were it not so, it could hardly be called a gift, which is not something that can be taken back – as those of you who have received it will understand!

Once the soul has become nothing, then God lives in her without ever breaking the peace he has given her, a peace that can neither be imagined nor described. The peace of his love is not the work of the body, or of the heart, or even of the spirit, because their observances have been overtaken by the divine work of Christ.

Our Lady is an example of this: she did not do the will of her senses, or even of her mind, but the will of God. This was, is and always will be her special way of understanding, loving and praising God: in all that she did she willed only the will of God, and so the life of glory was instilled directly into her mortal body.

Encouragement for those still subject to desires

(The Soul continues:) All you who are still subject to desires and have not yet found peace of mind, work hard at making yourselves nothing, as there is no rest for those who are always seeking it unless they first exhaust themselves. So give the virtues their due, with all the powers of your mind and will, till they have freed you from the debt you owe to Christ. As he himself said in the gospel: 'He who believes in me will also do the works that I do; and greater works than these will he do' (Jn 14:12). What does he mean by this? That only when the debt owed to Christ has been paid can you have the peace of oneness with God. May God bring you speedily to this peace, where you will find all the things your hearts at present desire in their natural state of perfection.

This state of natural perfection is a far cry from the state of those souls who have forgotten everything and been reduced to nothingness and enlightened, who have reached the highest state of being. There the soul is abandoned to God through him, with him and in him; there they no longer consciously praise or adore him, but do so only through what they cannot know or love or adore. Here their love is completely fulfilled and they have reached the final abandonment of their will. These two aspects do not contradict each other: the souls that can rest there have run their course; all that they do now is done through the goodness of God's will. And they can do whatever they please without making any return for God's gifts. Why shouldn't they? These gifts are also God himself, giving himself to these souls and changing them completely into him. He is Love and Love can do what she will, overcoming fear, discernment and reason. So these souls do not seek to understand fully but God puts full understanding into them.

CHAPTER EIGHT

The soul describes the seven stages

The first stage: keeping the commandments

I promised earlier to describe the seven stages in the ascent of the mountain from whose summit only God can be seen. This I shall now do and you should understand that each stage has its own time-span allotted to it.

The first stage is when a soul is touched by God's grace and set apart from sin, so that her will is set on keeping his commandments to the best of her ability. She sees, in fear and trembling, that God has commanded us to love him above all things and our neighbour as ourselves. This seems hard enough for her, enough work to keep her occupied for a thousand years, if she should live that long.

I was in this position once, I remember. Those of you who are still at this stage must not despair of moving on to higher stages. Be of good heart and have courage: faint hearts will not rise to tackle the demands of love. The faint-hearted take the lead in fear, not love, and do not allow God to work in them.

The second stage: following the counsel of perfection

The second stage is reached when the soul sees what counsels God gives those who would love him in a special way, beyond his commandments. And seeing this as a means of pleasing God, the soul like any good lover naturally wishes to please her Beloved. And so she sets out to follow the counsel of evangelical perfection, by mortifying her earthly desires and despising riches and honours, according to the example set by Jesus. She feels no bitterness in doing this, and no weakness in her body, but is sustained by the knowledge that God is leading her onwards and upwards.

The third stage: the death of the will

The third stage is reached when the soul looks carefully at the love she had developed for the works of perfection which have multiplied in her during the second stage. And what does this careful look tell her? That there is really nothing she can offer her Beloved except what he most loves, since other gifts are not really worthy of pure love. She sees her will attached to all good works and spiritual comforts, and then the truth is borne in on her that she must detach herself from just the perfections that grace has brought about in her, as these are precisely what she has to sacrifice to love. The sacrifice she is called to make is to abstain from all the good works which had in fact become her greatest pleasure.

So she abstains from all these good works that pleased her so much and puts her will which had become attached to the life of perfection to death. She seeks only to do the will of others and refuses all inclination of her own will, in order to destroy her own will. This is a very hard process – far more difficult than the two earlier stages. It is far harder to master the will of the spirit than it is to master the will of the body in order to do the will of the spirit. But this is what she has to do: break her will so as to leave more space where love can come to live in her. At this point she has to burden herself with the wills of others in order to free herself from the burden of herself.

The fourth stage: labours give way to contemplation

In the fourth stage, the soul is brought by love to delight in meditation alone, and abandons all labours outside her new task of contemplation, including doing the will of others. The soul is now in a highly delicate and even dangerous state, in which all she can bear is the touch of love's sheer delight. This she takes infinite pleasure in, and pride, out of the abundance of her love.

She now reveals the secrets of her heart, all the tenderness and sweetness of her love; she melts into the embrace of union from which she receives all love's delights. She is convinced there can be nothing higher than the life she now enjoys; love has given her such pleasure that she cannot believe God has anything higher to offer the soul than this love which Love has spread throughout her being.

It is indeed a wonderful thing for the soul to be taken up to these dizzy heights of love. She is in a drunken ecstasy of love and can see nothing but love; love sheds such a blinding light on her that she cannot see that there is a love surpassing even this. In this she is mistaken, for there are two stages beyond even this which can be attained in this life, but at this stage the soul is blinded by the onset of love, seizing her up into bliss as soon as she makes an approach, with a strength there is no resisting. So now the soul is taken up out of herself by a Love exceeding even the love she feels.

The fifth stage: the will abandoned to God

Now the soul sees what God is; that he IS, that all things come from him and that she herself is nothing, being not what is. So she feels an amazing humility at the thought of the infinite goodness of God giving her nothingness free will. She sees herself as nothing but wickedness, and yet with this wonderful gift of free will, this giving of being to what had none out of the pure goodness of God. Then such divine goodness is poured into the soul, in a ravishing flash of divine light, that she suddenly sees that she must remove this great gift of free will from anything that is not God, and never again place it where he is not.

Her will now sees by the spreading brightness of divine enlightenment, prompting her to put her will once more in God, which she cannot do without this divine enlightenment. Her will has to be detached from her own will so that it is given entirely to God. She now sees clearly her own nothingness, and indeed the wretchedness of her own nature, and sees, by divine enlightenment, that she has to will what is God's will for her without consciously willing it. This, in fact, is what she was given free will for. So she is separated from her will and her will from her. She gives it back to God, where it came from originally, in order to carry out the divine will, which cannot be carried out without the complete abandonment of all self-love. So there is no conflict of will left in her.

This gift of complete self-giving of her will brings her perfect peace, makes her the very being of love, nourished on the gift of love that gives her the pleasure of complete peace. There is no more conflict in her, since her will has been laid naked where it first came from, and where it belongs. As long as she withheld her will, she knew conflict; now she knows none.

The soul is now nothing, seeing her nothingness by the divine light that is in her; yet she knows everything, since the depth of her knowledge of her nothingness is such that it has no beginning and no end and cannot be measured. It is an immeasurable depth, but without being able to plumb this depth, she finds herself in it, which is something no one can do who has not reached this stage. The more she sees of herself, the more she realizes she cannot see the true extent of her wickedness. She sees herself naked in the darkest dungeon of sin. So she sees herself without the use of her sight: this is the utmost depth to which humility can attain, where there is no room for pride, since this total darkness shows her herself with total clarity.

This is the lowest point the soul can reach, and from this lowest point she is able to look up and clearly see the sun of God's goodness through the light of his divine favour, and this goodness draws her out of herself into itself, where she is united to the divine goodness itself. This happens through her knowledge of the two natures: the infinite goodness of God and the wickedness of her own mis-spent youth. But now mercy has joined forces with justice and brought this soul to his goodness, where she is everything and nothing, since she is one with the Beloved.

So the soul has fallen from the state of love to that of nothingness, without which she cannot be everything. Taken rightly, this fall is so precious to her that she cannot and should not rise from the depths into which she has fallen. She must stay there, accepting the loss of joy of the spirit that before took pride in its goodness and is now totally humbled. In the fourth stage, her will took her fine and free to the heights of contemplation, but in this fifth she sees herself clearly, no longer blinded by love. It is now her knowledge of God's goodness that gives her life, and this leads her to renounce herself, and having done this she is free from all slaveries and possesses complete freedom of being, relieved of all pressures.

The sixth stage: freedom in enlightenment

In the sixth stage the soul no longer sees her own nothingness from the depths of humility, nor the greatness of God through his great goodness. Instead, God sees himself in her through his own power, enlightens her himself, so that she sees that nothing exists save God alone, the source of all being. What is, is God, and the soul sees nothing but God, because whoever sees this of God, sees God. So in this sixth stage the soul is free, purified and enlightened, but not yet glorified, because glory belongs to the seventh stage, which is the glory of heaven of which no one can speak.

Pure and enlightened, it is no longer her seeing God and herself, but God seeing himself in her, through her and outside her, and showing her that there is nothing other than God. She knows nothing except him, loves nothing except him, and praises nothing except him: how could she, when there is nothing except him? Whatever exists does so through his goodness, so she loves his goodness which he has been so good as to give her, this goodness which is in God himself. God cannot abandon his goodness; he is what his goodness gives, and goodness is what he is. So by his great goodness, she sees his goodness, through the divine light which enlightens the soul at this sixth stage.

There is nothing except what he is, and she sees the reality of his divine power through being united to the love of his goodness. She sees this in him and with him, the unmade maker, without going through anything that belongs to her senses. She sees that all is in the being of God, and this sixth stage is seeing the being of God, who is love and has paid all debts.

The seventh stage

The seventh stage cannot be described. God reserves it to himself, and will give it to us in his everlasting glory. We cannot know it in this life, but only when our soul has left our body.

PART THREE

The author speaks
through the soul

CHAPTER NINE

The soul describes her own progress

Our Lady's special graces and what the 'damaged' must see

Mary, our blessed Lady, you had more perfect grace in you from the time you were conceived in your mother's womb than did the twelve apostles when they received the light of the Holy Spirit at Pentecost! This was indeed necessary, for if God the Son had found so much as the least spot or stain of vanity in you, he could not have chosen you to be his mother; yet you were his mother, and no such spot or stain could have been in you.

I see our Lady standing at the foot of the Cross, where Jesus suffered for the fault of Adam, repairing more than was damaged by the original fault, bringing a new life of grace which our Lady had in the wholeness of her being.

What would you have said to those whose cruelty caused this suffering? How would you have repaid them for their sin? If needs be, you would have given your own life rather than know God could not forgive them their sin. But this was not necessary, as Christ re-united man to God in such abundance and such anguish.

In such abundance, because the tiniest drop of his

blood, that would sit on the point of a needle, would have been enough to redeem a hundred thousand worlds, had there been so many. But he gave his blood in such abundance that it has detached me from myself and made me live in accordance with the divine will.

In such anguish, that if all the pains suffered by the human race from the time of Adam till the end of the world were to be united in one being, they would be but the tiniest part of what our Lord Jesus Christ suffered in his person.

Then I saw this, that the divine nature became one with our nature for our sakes in the person of God the Son. What a thought this is! If God had not willed it, how could anyone expect Jesus Christ to be poor and rejected and to suffer for us? What a wonderful work of love constrained him to suffer thus for us, since he had taken on our nature in which to suffer and die! He could only do this because the divine nature took on human nature and united us with God in the person of his Son. This thought alone is enough to set us free from cares if we will only allow it to work in us. I did not allow it to: he would have set me free the moment I first had this thought, but I would not allow this to happen. What an irreparable loss! I held foolishly to my own views and tried to do my own works, and the result was that I did nothing. Then I saw that he who was both God and man was despised and rejected by man just for me, to my shame. And I saw that his poverty was for me, and that he died for me: to see these things clearly is to understand everything.

You who are the Way, the Truth and the Life, it is

better for us to think of one of the great benefits you
have brought us; it will set out hearts more firmly in
your love, than if the whole of earth and heaven were
given up to be burned.

Then I saw his beauty and truth, and truth told me
that I should not see the Trinity till my soul had
become as free from sin as the soul of Jesus. Jesus' soul
was glorified from the moment it was made by the
Trinity and made one with human and divine nature
in the person of the Son, and since the soul was united
to the divine nature, the mortal body could commit no
sin.

Then I saw who would go to heaven. Truth told me
that only those whose lives mirrored that of the Son of
God himself would be saved. This means that those
who are to be saved are those who have become God's
sons through his grace, those of whom he said: 'Here
are my mother and my brethren! For whoever does
the will of my Father in heaven is my brother, and
sister, and mother' (Mt. 12. 50).

Then I saw the seraphim and asked them why
God's love had made the Son become man for us, and
why we had been made, and about all God's
continuing goodness to his creatures. And Love
answered me and said that all that has been done was
done so that the will of the Trinity might be fulfilled.
This is a wonderful and profitable thing to see, and if
you think about it, it will remove all cares from you
and set you on the road to the perfection we have been
talking about.

There are seven things that the 'damaged' can
meditate on with profit: the Apostles, St Mary

Magdalen, St John the Baptist, the Virgin Mary, the union of divine and human nature in the person of the Son, how Christ suffered for us in his human nature, and how the seraphim are part of the divine will.

What I saw in the life of the spirit

Now let me tell you what I saw while I was in the life of the spirit: I saw God in me and myself in him, and I felt great desire for him. These three things were then my being, though I now know that there can be little peace for those who still feel desires. I did not know how to cope with my feeling of God being in me, and of my being in God, till I began to meditate on these lines, and this taught me how:

– Lord God, I do not know what your eternal power, eternal wisdom and eternal goodnes can mean, so I do not know what you are;

– Lord God, I do not know what I am, because I cannot realize my absolute weakness, foolishness and wickedness;

– Lord, you are all goodness, from the overflowing divine goodness that is all in you, and I am all wickedness, from the overflowing wickedness that is all in me;

– Lord, you are all power and wisdom and goodness, with no beginning, beyond understanding and without end; I am all weakness, foolishness and wickedness, with no beginning, beyond understanding and beyond measure;

– Lord, you alone are one God in three persons; I am your one enemy in three miseries;

– Lord, you are Father, Son and Holy Spirit; I am weakness, folly and wickedness;

– Lord, I can grasp your power and wisdom and goodness as much as I can grasp my weakness, folly and wickedness;

– Lord, I can grasp my own weakness, folly and wickedness as much as I can grasp your power and wisdom and goodness. If I could understand one of these two natures, then I could understand both. This is the test, and just as I cannot grasp the extent of my wickedness compared to what it is, so I cannot grasp the extent of your goodness compared to what it is. But the little I do understand of my wickedness gives me what understanding I do have of your goodness. This is indeed so little that there is no describing it, since it is nothing compared to what I cannot understand. So all I can say is that you *are*, and that there is nothing else.

Meditation resulting from seeing my
wickedness and his goodness

When I had seen all these things, I began to see how I might find favour with him who is all goodness, despite my being all wickedness. I began to meditate on the need to mould my will to his, without seeking favours in return, and my meditation went like this:

– If you would rather I had never existed, so that I could never have offended you, then so would I;

– If you wish to send me all the torments you can to avenge my faults, then this is what I want;

– If I could be like you, without fault, and then suffer

the poverty and humiliation and pain that Christ did, out of his goodness and wisdom and power, then I should like to be;

– If I could be as worthy in myself as you are in yourself, so that none of my worth could be taken from me without my willing it to be, then I should place all this worth in you and become nothing rather than keep anything of myself that did not come from you;

– If all this worth belonged to me of right, then I should rather lose it all beyond hope of recovery than have it when it did not come from you. And if I had all the torments you can send, then I should prefer these to any glory that did not come from you, even though it might last for ever;

– Rather than do anything to displease you, I should prefer to see your human nature suffering on the Cross as much as you did suffer for me – so much do I not want to displease you;

– If I knew that the whole of your creation, myself included, would be destroyed unless I offended against his will, then I would rather see it destroyed;

– If I knew that I would have such everlasting torment as you have everlasting goodness unless I offended you, then I would choose the everlasting torment rather than offend you;

– If you were to give me as much of your goodness as you have everlasting value, I should value it only for your sake; if I lost it, I should lament the loss only for your sake; if you gave it back to me, I should rejoice in it only for your sake. And if you would rather I became nothing than received your goodness, then nothing it shall be;

– If it were possible for me to have as much of you in me as you have in yourself, and if I saw that it would please you better for me to suffer as much as you are good, then I would rather have the sufferings than you in me;

– If I knew that Jesus in his manhood and the Virgin Mary and all the saints in heaven were pleading that I should have you in me rather than the sufferings, and you were to say to me: 'I will give you the gift of my being in you, if you want it, because these my friends in heaven have pleaded with me, but without their pleading I would not be giving it to you; so if you want it, take it!', then I would suffer the torments for ever rather than take this gift from you knowing it did not come from your will alone. If the humanity of Christ, and the Virgin Mary, and all the saints prayed for it to be given to me, I would not have it unless it came from the sheer goodness and goodwill and love that a lover has for his love;

– Suppose you wanted me to love someone else more than you (words fail me, but I must go on) – I cannot say that I would, this is something I must think about;

– Suppose you wanted to love someone else more than you love me (words fail me again at the thought) – I have no answer because I know I can't wish for this;

– Suppose you wanted someone else to love me more than you do (words fail me again) – again I have no answer; I shall have to think about it.

And so I did, and I told him that these last three were very hard, far harder to conceive and consent to than all the others, and I did not see how I could possibly want any of these things. And he still pushed me to answer, and because I still loved myself as well as him, I could not see clearly and this caused me great distress. No one who has not been put to the test in this way can understand this. And I was to know no peace until I could find an answer to these things.

Oh, yes, I still loved myself, and so I could not answer. If I had not still loved myself, I could have answered in a flash, and so saved myself all the distress that came from not losing myself in him.

The surrender of love and will

How hard the answer is! If I knew that he would go away from me after all the favours his love had brought me, I might be able to endure the thought, but to think that it could be just a game of chance, that he could want to simply when he wanted to and just because he wanted to . . . ! But I found my answer and said:

– Lord, even if this change should come about in fact, as we are now only supposing, I still love you for yourself and in yourself. So for your sake I did not desire this change. If I could do my will as well as the will you have given me, and if you had made me like you in all things except that I could change my will for one other than the will you have given me, then I would find any of these things very difficult, since they would not be coming from your goodness alone. But if I knew beyond all doubt that they came from your will without any diminishing of your goodness, then I should accept them all without further question, and this is where my will comes to an end.

148

– Lord, I hereby surrender my will and my love; you have brought them to the point of surrender. I had thought that my calling was always to live in love through the promptings of my will. But now both love and will – which brought me out of my spiritual childhood – are dead in me, and in this death I find my freedom.

Then Justice came to me and asked how he could spare me any of the sufferings that might be due to me; and Mercy came and asked if she could help. And I told them that I had no further need of either of them.

Then Love came to me full of goodness, Love who had so often forced me out of my mind and consumed me in her fires, and told me that she held all things that have been and are to come in her goodness; that I could take what I wanted from her and that if I wanted all of her, then that was what she wanted too. She said that my will was her will and that therefore I should take my will. And I told her that I was sheer nothingness, so how could I want anything? I can want nothing that does not come from the goodness of God, but everything that is in him is fulfilled in him and so nothing exists that does not come from him, and so I am totally lost in him.

So the end of this trial of my youth and former high spirits was the surrender of my will and all that I did of myself, and of the love that formerly gladdened my heart. This came about through a sudden divine illumination that gave me a glimpse of the truth, showed me himself as he is and myself as I am, him so high and me so low that I could only stay helpless where I was. And I saw that this was for the best. If you cannot understand this, I am sorry, but there is no other way to express it. It is a miraculous work of God's, and the soul must not complain of it.

The love felt in the life of the spirit compared to wanting nothing

I have given you an explanation of how I sought to free myself from cares and to find the way forward from my damaged state. The love that I felt in my spirit was in effect a sign of being still 'damaged', since these tender feelings of affection in the spirit are in fact the work of the spirit, though the soul in this state thinks they are God's work in her, and in staying so attached to them, she is staying attached to herself, though she cannot see this. And this love that comes from tender feelings is not clear knowledge, and so is open to deception; it is the youthful love that seeks to express itself in works, and cannot be surpassed as long as these feelings of affection remain in the spirit.

This is a long way from the life of true freedom, which is governed by wanting nothing. This wanting nothing is the ground in which the seed of divinity, which never perishes, can be sown, but few people prepare their ground to receive this seed.

There are many who are 'perished' in affection, and many who stay 'damaged' in the life of the spirit, relying on works of virtue and good will. But there are few who come through to the life of freedom that never fails, which this book has described, who have only the will that pure love gives them, since pure love gives one will and one love, one love that is wholly and utterly pure in the state of divine love, always wholly united to the divine will. Those that reach this stage are made nothing, and this matters nothing to them, since they are but God's work and God's work can never be less than everything to them.

If they try to do their own work, they are working for themselves; whereas once they are made nothing, they cannot work for themselves. And since God's work cannot grow less, they cannot grow weary of God's work, unless they try to replace it with their own. If they try to do this, then they are trying to act for themselves, and once they have become nothing, there is nothing they can do this with.

The soul becomes herself by becoming nothing, and once she has gone out of herself and become nothing, she has true knowledge of the gifts of God through the miracle of his gift to her, which she receives in faith.

The highest perfection of the soul

The soul at the highest stage of her perfection and nearest the dark night is beyond noticing the rules of the Church. She is commanded by pure love, which is a higher mistress than what we call 'charitable works'. She has passed so far beyond the works of virtue that she no longer knows what they are about – but yet she has assimilated them to the point where they are part of her and obey her intrinsically. Because they are part of her, the Church cannot control her – the Church here being understood as mainly to do with those who live in the fear of the Lord, which is one of the gifts of the Holy Spirit. But this fear of the Lord can be a disturbing influence in the life of complete freedom.

The free soul has no further need of fear of the Lord, since she has gone beyond both the pleasures of the body and the will of the spirit and has placed her whole will in the dark night, taking no account of herself or her nothingness. The 'greater part' has paid any debt she owed our Lord; she owes him nothing, however great her debt may have been. The 'greater part' has shown her what her 'lesser part' owed – but you need to have full faith, not just the sense of knowing, if you are to be sure of this: it is easy to deceive oneself through the affection of the spirit, which works against clear knowledge and prevents one from realizing the deepest sense of this ransom from debt, and from trusting fully in God's goodness, relying instead on one's own works.

What a deception this is! However good a creature's works, they are nothing compared to God's goodness; his wisdom gives his goodness to souls only for his own goodness' sake: new goodness can only grow through understanding his goodness in this way.

God's goodness and the union between God and the soul

God's goodness is worth more than anyone can do in a hundred thousand years or anything the Church can do in history. The highest point of his goodness is the most accessible, in that it takes the soul into himself and makes her always one with his will, whatever may happen to her. Made no one in this one, she is without fear and without joy; she has no more to do for God than he has to do for her, since she is nothing and he is everything. This is enough for her, the fact that he *is*; knowing this, she need hold nothing of herself back in making herself nothing. And nothing she is: back where she was before she had being. Everything she has is from God, and she is what God is, and was, and what she was before God made her, in union with him.

In this state she can no more pray than she did before she was made, since all she has comes from God's goodness, from the will of his love in the soft dark night. So she cannot pray. She now hates most what she most loved before, but has no less love on account of this. She has held nothing back; she has no space in which to live, and occupying no space, has nowhere to love herself – as is obvious! She is forbidden to work: all she must do is exist in God, become perfectly one with him, as Jesus prayed for his disciples.

This is the goal of those who take no care for themselves, since love provides everything for them, even in their dealings with their fellow Christians. And so they can say:

It is truly right and just for all things to call me holy, as all things were made for me, and I can take them as mine of right.

For you, Lord, have loved me as Father, in all your everlasting power;

For you, Lord, have loved me as Son, in all your everlasting wisdom, and in all your goodness, as a friend.

So now I can say that you love no one more than

me, because just as your infinite goodness allows your
most blessed mother and all the angels and saints to
enjoy the glorious blessings of your infinite goodness
to an extent beyond what they deserve, so your infinite
goodness will not allow me to suffer what I deserve,
but will give me as much of your continual favour as I
would have of suffering without your infinite
goodness. This is the meaning of this song:

This is why he looks on me
and loves no one more than me –
  the essence of my heart.

This is why he looks on me:
this is all he wants to be –
  made one with my being.

This is why he looks on me
and loves no one more than me –
  he is all I need.

This is why he looks on me:
I want what he wants for me –
  Love to win my heart.

This is why he looks on me
and loves no one more than me –
  he whom I delight in seeing.

This is why he looks on me:
His will is what mine must be –
  No other shall I need.

This is why he looks on me
and loves no one more than me.

The soul describes the seven stages

And now: *Amen*

This is the end of the book I have called
A Mirror for Simple Souls.

Translator's Epilogue

Oh most glorious Trinity, source of all goodness,
    thy will be done
    on earth as it is in heaven.
Oh dearest Lord, I give you thanks with all my heart for all your gifts to me, your humble and unworthy servant, and most particularly for allowing me, a most unsuitable person, to translate this book. And thanks and praise to you for having enabled me to finish it, which I never could have done without your grace. To you be praise and honour and glory, for this and all good works.

    I entreat you, almighty God, guide those who read this book, so that they will understand it all; give them the grace to take it in the sense it is meant; let your Holy Spirit come upon them and give them the love to understand it as your Spirit of Love wrote it, to your honour and their benefit through your everlasting goodness.

    Have mercy on me, a sinner, Lord, have mercy.
    All glory, praise and honour to you, almighty Lord,
    For ever and ever,
    Amen.

SPIRITUAL CLASSICS
Some other titles in the series

A LETTER OF PRIVATE DIRECTION

and other treatises by a fourteenth-century English Mystic. A lively new translation of the *Book of Prive Counseling* and the same author's *Mystical Theology* and *The Way to true Contemplation* or *Benjamin*. This is a collection of connected texts by the author of the *Cloud of Unknowing*, written for contemplatives who want to divest themselves of everything that stands in the way of divine love. With dramatic force, vigorous language yet tender friendship, the author conducts the reader towards the true life and love offered by the mystical experience, teaching self-analysis on the way to self-denial, and constantly reinforcing the simple yet profound message that God *is* love.

A LETTER FROM JESUS CHRIST

by John of Landsberg. A new version of the sixteenth-century *Epistle of Jesus Christ to the Soul* by Johannes Lanspergius which brings out admirably the author's psychological accuracy and power of spiritual direction. He couches his advice in the form of a letter of information and encouragement written directly by Jesus to the individual soul. The emphasis is on humility and self-denial, on how to know oneself and how to reach a true piety in a world which helps one's own inclinations to interrupt the search for perfection.

THE CELL OF SELF-KNOWLEDGE

Early English mystical treatises. A straightforward new version of the major texts in the famous traditional collection published by Henry Pepwell in 1521 and long established as a varied guide to the spiritual life. Among the works included are *Our Lord's Treatise on Contemplation* by the colourful and racy lay mystic Margery Kempe; *Profitable Teachings from the life of St Catherine*; the *Song of Angels*, by Walter Hilton, author of *The Ladder of Perfection*; *The Letter of Prayer*, *Moderation in Spiritual Impulses* and *The Discerning of Spirits*, all by the author of *The Cloud of Unknowing*.

242

French mystic
mirror for

100417

Class No. 242 ...... Acc. No. ....

COLÁISTE OIDEACHAIS
MHUIRE GAN SMÁL,
LUIMNEACH.